BILAKHULU !

BILAKHULU !

LONGER POEMS

Vonani Bila

For my wife Gudani and our beautiful children
Mhlahlandlela, Samora and Masase

In memory of my father
Risimati Daniel Bila

The son of Dayimani
wa Jonas
wa Makhayingi
wa Mpfumari
wa Xanjhinghu
wa Ntshovi
wa Xisilafole xi nga ri na nhonga xi sila hi mandla
Bilakhulu!
Msengana
Bilakhulu!
Mhlahlandlela

ISBN: 978-0-9870282-5-9
ebook ISBN: 978-1-928476-21-4

Deep South
contact@deepsouth.co.za
www.deepsouth.co.za

Distributed in South Africa by
University of KwaZulu-Natal Press
www.ukznpress.co.za

Distributed worldwide by
African Books Collective
PO Box 721, Oxford, OX1 9EN, UK
www.africanbookscollective.com/publishers/deep-south

Deep South acknowledges the financial assistance of
the National Arts Council for the production of this book

NATIONAL ARTS COUNCIL
OF SOUTH AFRICA

Cover design: Liz Gowans and Robert Berold
Text design and layout: Liz Gowans

Cover etching: Colbert Mashile, *Paesekele se Robege*, 2008

CONTENTS

Images from childhood

i

the people of pfukani
whose huts were uprooted in 1968
grass-thatched roofs loaded in gg trucks
goats, dogs, bicycles and pots heaped onto the trucks
poor people trekking to the unknown barren land
leaving behind fruit trees and gardens
leaving behind graves of their beloved ones
trekking to gandlanani, squashed like sardines
vavanuna va xandile na maburuku   (men's pants back to front)
vavasati va xandile na swikete   (women's skirts back to front)
hi xibububu xo pfuxiwa hi huwa ya tilori   (woken up hurriedly by the
                                                                             roaring trucks)
because it was time
to separate vhavenda from vatsonga
because it was time
to make way for the white man.

ii

shirley primary
the same school where eduardo mondlane taught
boys used to play, jumping over the dump
jumping over the blazing fire
but i can't forget that day
when oriel tried to jump over the fire
whether he tripped or was pushed into the burning flames i don't know
but his clothes caught fire
his hair caught fire
clothes and flesh became one
everyone thought it was the end of him.

iii

i remember
my mother making fire in the open ground
stirring the bubbling pot of pap amidst cracking thunder
pelting rain and flashing lightning
even in our windowless huts
we sailed, floating in water on the mats
when grass-thatched huts caved in to bucketing rains.

iv

winter days at lemana high
white teachers opened windows
for the chilly air to freeze our toes
the same teachers who were paid
a tolerance bonus to teach a black child.

v

the wooden electric pole behind our house
planted in the family cemetery
cables of fire trapping swallows and owls
turning mischievous monkeys green
cables of modern fire that galloped kilometres from town
to supply a certain dombani, victor, magantawa
and bernard with warmth
bypassing our darknesss and the smog.

vi

the graves under water
the colossal deep dam of death
that the big man dombani built
where we swam naked in summer
our rags drying in thorn trees

i remember
dombani the hefty burly-surly man
clad in khaki wear and veldskoene
the man with a bloodthirsty temper
wielding a rifle
on horseback
at sunset
cracking shots in the air
reptiles and porcupines retreating to holes
riding around the dam
watching for the black boy
to raise his head above water
to fire with delight
to crack the boy's skull
to halt his breath
or to just see the little boy consumed by water
to teach him a lesson
that under the orbiting sun
the dam is not for naked black boys
it's not for a speck of village dust
but it's for sailing white men in boats
who catch fish
even when drunk.

N'wa-yingwani

n'wa-yingwani
your only son xiringa left elim in the riotous 80s
a white farmer was found dead
body parts chopped to pieces
flesh stuffed in a black body bag
& thrown into the levubu river
but the hungry crocodiles
shook their heads
let the white man float away

we are told
the farmer slapped xiringa's aunt maria
that boy who she carried on her back
on the same farm years ago
but the boer boy forgot who'd wiped his soiled backside
he set the dogs on maria
after she asked for permission
to bury her grandmother
in the village

so when xiringa heard the news
of his aunt's death from the jaws of pit-bull dogs
he walked in the hazy night
brandishing his axe & okapi knife
he walked from valdezia village to levubu farm
to slice through the pale flesh
because the white man had to pay
for his sins & those of his forefathers

n'wa-yingwani
the green flies put a price tag on xiringa's head
wanted: dead or alive
they searched for him in the mashau mountains
in the mambila caves

& the bush below the deep flowing albasini dam
that's where he was arrested, after a week
but he had long shaved his head & beard so clean
chewed *phunyuka bamphethe*
that's why even in court it was stinking
for he had oiled his body with *phala bashimane* muthi
the judge fell asleep & let him walk free
xiringa couldn't work on farms anymore
he fled to the tautona gold mine in carletonville
west of jozi-mjipa-msawawa
he left guva the wife waiting
to be serviced by night angels
because he only returned home on good friday & december
to plant seeds

n'wa-yingwani
your son toiled under the belly of the dark earth
crawling, digging the gold in collapsing mine tunnels
sweating in the deep, dark & damp tunnels
madalasite
colliding with the big biting rats in dusty tunnels
hoping the flashlight on the helmet wouldn't die
fingers freezing in the winter so cold in tunnels
breathing leaks of gases so deadly in tunnels
ankle deep in muddy water, up & down in tunnels
extracting the ounce of gold for the white man
stamping on skulls of ghosts that live in tunnels
that's where your son sucked the silica dust
the dust that weakened his lungs
muchochaphansi

n'wa-yingwani
your son lived in cramped hostel living quarters
cracking sounds of kwaito from friday to sunday
cash begging mamas in pleated skirts
keeping vigil in men's hostels

when his hormone-relieving machine started to stutter
he would drink *imbiza* to cure any sign of gonorrhoea
& at dawn on friday morning, he would drink gallons of warm water
& throw it away, groaning like a bull
he'd drink the bitter aloe juice
& cheap chinese sex tablets to boost his body
then he would brag about knocking three girls a day
without a rubber
at month end, he would fill up the table with black label
dance to blasting sounds with trousers dangling
then he would retire to the living quarters
pockets full of holes
grovelling

n'wa-yingwani
when your son was retrenched
he moved to the bright lights of jozi
he stood over the glinting high-rise building
like a discerning man and declared:
hillbrow is awash with fresh swaying roses
beetle-like rural girls use cowdung as body lotion
xiringa the cock-eyed miner returned home dissolved
girls with darting eyes
at high-rise hillbrow's little roseneath melted his heart
girls in skimpy wear flaunting their assets
at the moulin rouge hotel melted his heart
xiringa loved girls winking at him at the summit & ambassador
disco girls bingeing & smoking weed at the royal hotel
strip-teasers in cubicles at the diplomat hotel
those thighs re-birthed him everytime
& the bottle fed the newborn
at high-rise hillbrow

n'wa-yingwani
lust withered xiringa's heart
he returned to lean on guva the village wife, broke & broken

once a ubiquitous *pantsula* of flair
he came home a mere bundle of bones
wearing thrush and tuberculosis
he came home, a parcel loaded in city to city bus to valdezia
he returned to be changed soiled nappies
because he couldn't eat a sweet with its wrapper
in fast-paced joburg
he returned to guva the hospice
but he had long pumped her with the poison of a social virus
he returned wheelchair-bound to die
without any azt-virodene-arv solvent
because he roamed around hillbrow's pubs, brothels & disco joints
where de kok's askari hordes planted the aids landmine
in desperate girls

n'wa-yingwani
when guva fell ill, some people called her a *cabbage*
because she'd been born prematurely
mbeki gave her an aids pension
n'wa-yingwani, you bathed her
changed her soiled nappies, wiped her vomit
& slimy foam around the mouth
you carried her feeble frame on your back to the pension pay-point
sometimes you'd push her, fastened on a green wheelbarrow
manto's *ubhejana*, garlic, beetroot, ginger
& lemon couldn't straighten her legs
not even drinking and washing
with the urine of a donkey
could revitalize her scorched face
oh guva, beautiful woman, why don't the medics give her an anesthesia
so that she could be free from the bucket for emergency
behind the door?

n'wa-yingwani
mbeki might never have seen an aids grave
but here in this village

the day slips into night so quick
& in the early hours of the morning
the young ones line up to fill up fresh open graves

n'wa-yingwani
every time you see your sick grandchildren
tears well down your cheeks
your heart has borne the weight of pain
your son died in your hands, at dusk
on the zigzagging dirt path to elim hospital
after just six months of returning home
now your daughter-in-law is packing up
she tried to take a shower in a plastic basin
to clean away the pungent smell of aids
but the death monster groans feverishly in her lungs

n'wa-yingwani
your two grandchildren on arvs
will soon vanish like doves in the night
but when the tree is uprooted like that
where will children so young find a branch to rest their hopes on
to shelter secrets of adulthood...?

oh, n'wa-yingwani
you weep tearlessly in a hospital bed
stretched & worn-out
frothy & skeletal frame wired with drips and tubes
the clock ticks slowly
the doctor checks the colour of your urine:
you've got high blood & you are hiv-positive mama
i look into your sunken eyes
& the weary look you wear
& the furrow lining your brow
a cluster of glistening *xirimela* dims
i hold your cold hand & feel the heavy silence
death is in your throat here at giyani block

brown clouds hang in the burning air
a tent is planted in your yard
the elderly women in black line up on mats
how will they announce the dreaded news to your tearful infants
your ailing, yelling grandchildren?
because no-one can get used to this daily death
again, shovels clatter
& we shove & shuffle facing the tomb

Why I am not a teacher

Thanks Robert Berold and Frank O'Hara

I am not a teacher. but I studied
to be one at my blacks only college.
I specialised in Economics and Business Economics
in third year I got distinctions in these subjects
but we didn't have a spaza shop at home to practice my economics

those days, the early 90s, students at Tivumbeni College
were guarded by fully armed soldiers
they stood erect by the classroom door with their dogs
they were on duty, to protect the white lecturers and spies among us

those days, our list of demands was long:
fight bantu education. free education for all. change the college menu.
fight the mosquitoes in hostels and on campus.
reinstate expelled students.
allow pregnant women to study. allow unions to operate on campus.
release the detained students whose balls we hear
are being squeezed in Pietersburg prison

our stomachs and necks were mammoth
from eating mountains of pap, chunks of kudu meat and cabbage
on Sundays we ate penguins disguised as chicken
some would queue at the toilet
because sometimes that food was a laxative
but my stomach was as tough as Thabazimbi steel

those days, it was necessary to march
even to be chased away from the campus for weeks
we wanted to be nourished by eating rice, fresh fish and salad
we wanted English breakfast, yoghurt, cereal and fruits
essential food for teachers who didn't eat everyday at home

we were not always angry
on Fridays we demanded to watch blue movies
enjoyed disco at the main hall
we wanted more money for liquor for our freshers' ball
yes, we wanted to be complete teachers

we threw stones against ready-to-shoot soldiers and their ugly casspirs
dustbin lids were our shields
we knew that to jump over barbed wire
could tear our shirts and trousers
but we were at war with dogs

the old men and women students were cowards
they didn't like to toyi toyi or throw stones
they had left their partners and children back home
they were at college to learn
but learn what?

those days, the 90s, we slept in hostels
on old shaking mattresses that sank like ships
if one student caught flu, all of us would cough and sneeze
in summer we removed our beds, slept outside
mosquitoes loved the blood of first years especially

we wanted to share hostels with female students
but no man was allowed at the females' hostel after 12 midnight
that was prison
to be accommodated in separate camps

I hated our showers –
this one guy would wake up too early to take a shower
but would finish after an hour
if you peeped through the shower door
you would see him rubbing his dick hard and fast with Sunlight soap
you would hear him scream softly, then madly and loudly
S'bongile! Si-bo-ngi-le! Sibongi-lee!

many students were too poor –
some depended on the cash from selling corn beer or even dagga
some on cash from annual sales of goats and cattle and pigs
in first year, I only had one pair of trousers
and one pair of police shoes, from Philly my brother
and a t-shirt with the words:
Nkosi Sikelele iAfrika

I felt I could only teach in Gazankulu or Venda
couldn't dream of teaching the township kids in Pretoria or Soweto
couldn't stand teaching coconuts who knew English
better than their teacher
that's why I am not a teacher

there were border industries in Nkowankowa
men and women from Dan and Lusaka villages worked there
we never visited these firms like Busaf
but we were studying Business Economics
from 7.30am to 1pm, we repeated high school Economics

I wished the governor of the Reserve Bank
would give us a talk at college
or Mbhazima Shilowa come tell us about trade unions and scab labour
I wished someone from the PAC or Azapo would tell us
why blacks were landless
why they worked on farms in Tzaneen
and mines in Phalaborwa and Musina
to generate the wealth they didn't own

I came to college to be a smart teacher:
to understand the public budget
and why so little was reaching to so-called reserves
I wanted to understand the country's debt
and the odious apartheid debt
why there's no water in Elim when I'm told
there's a pipeline from Joao Albasini Dam that passes through Elim

to supply whites in Louis Trichardt

I was a new teacher with a certificate
Those days new teachers got jobs far away in Bushbuckridge
but I was lucky, I got my job at Ongedagte High
in Ekurhuleni near Elim
on Sunday I went to my new family with pots, plates,
paraffin stove and blankets
a beautiful girl swept my room
then she brought a tray full of pap and *miroho*

the principal wanted me to teach Accounting from grade 8 to grade 12
I told him I got F in Accounting in matric
I couldn't teach something I don't know
so I resigned on my first day as a teacher
I asked Vivien my classmate who specialised in Accounting
to take my post
then I came home with my pots, paraffin stove and blankets
leaving my empty hut and its fresh cowdung floor

Boys from Seshego

you loiter through polokwane town
knock at doors of our apartments and offices
with darting eyes
you monitor every movement of tenants
a shit job you have created for yourselves
a job that only requires
the ability to ashamedly, carelessly
instil fear & fever
in your defenceless victim
with a sharp blade
& a coughing metal

you clean shaven heads from seshego
in sneakers, jeans & hats
you crawl like crabs
or walk as if the earth is layered with eggs
you like it when the clouds brood
in streaming rains
especially in the night
wearing balaclavas & gloves
you check curtains of bedrooms & kitchens
sprinkle muthi, burn muthi
you do your job unhindered
not even dogs bark at you
no shadows follow you
& no police can trace
your fingerprints or footprints
all washed away by rain
& dew of the night

on may day
red t-shirt clad workers
sing & dance in squares and streets
as they celebrate the right to strike

& a living wage
but you, a merciless brigade
you enter suburb after suburb
house after house
shack after shack
you shepherd the workers, your sheep
& shear their wool in winter
you strike like serpents
you search and find doors even in the dark
like slithering serpents
serpents from the sprawling township of delirium
of coughing lungs & aids-ravaged frames
of cracked-lipped children
crammed in dark matchbox walls
in incestuous aging beds
you don't sleep in winter
you roam, buzz around our dreams of hysteria
scare us with swords, pangas & guns

boys from seshego, you should be on scaffolds – rebuilding the city
you should be on farms – tilling the land
or growing crops to feed this starving nation
boys, you should be in universities sucking knowledge & skills
teaching the illiterate nation to read & write
boys, you should be on the roadside
fixing the potholes, mapping the road & bridge to mtititi
boys, you should be saving lives
that crumble like mud huts
in decaying hospitals
but here you are, scar-faced
forever drunk
with deadened hearts
when it's cold & dark
normal human beings fast asleep
pulling the blanket that way & this way
you break burglar doors

with crowbars and chisels
flat screens, touch screen cellphones, dvd players,
laptops, cash, clothing – your loot
you even finish off the left-over food
sell stolen goods to second-hand shops
for next to nothing
sometimes you even sell mine back to me
in the street

march 2012: at lerato's place, apartment number 7
you took liquor from the fridge
sat on the sofas & opened beer with your teeth
& drank leisurely
then, you prepared a meal
pap, mutton & gravy
the couple and their son had locked themselves
in their bedroom
"we heard them when they came in,
we heard the noise as they ransacked
& combed the cupboards in the sitting room
we heard the noise & their drunken laughter
as howling prowlers grabbed the tv sets & emptied the jewelry box
& when my sleep-walking husband woke up from his dreams
he pulled out an iron rod
a pepper spray in hand
i held his hand tightly:
'matome, you are not going to do silly things
these stone-hearted thieves are armed to the teeth
they'll haul & drag me like an animal
drop their pants & devour me
before they slit your throat in your pyjamas
do you want to become garbage –
a pile of frozen worms?
you'll be lucky if these mindless wolves
leave you to stumble on crutches
please listen to me my love

these scumbags might put our only toddler in a bag
sell him at a baby auction
i'm too young to be a widow
to carry a void in my heart'
so the boys with river-like zigzagging scars
took what they wanted in the sitting room
then they knocked at our room
tried to open the door
we pushed back the door
screaming, help, help!
my husband with a pepper spray, trembling
we tried to call the police
but the boys vanished in the rain
before the men in uniform could come
after an hour
from just three kilometres away
& all they did was to take down
the statement
'so the boys didn't rape you?' they asked
& laughed at my urine-wet night gown"

may 2008: burglars climbed into the roof
of the president's official mahlambandlopfu residence
in government avenue
right in the capital city, pretoria
closed circuit television cameras watching
they walked away with the aluminium wire

                    *

april 2012: you thugs with delirium were here again
here at ritruda number 12
you knew i live alone
you knew i go home to elim
you came
used crowbars to try to break in

but the bila gods held the door too tight
i only came back to finish your job
broke into my own house
because i needed to enter
& my neighbours who sleep in the sitting room
beside the window
just a few centimetres from my door
simply didn't hear a thing
though they drink the whole night
& sleep in the morning
or they didn't want to be witnesses in court
or perhaps they work with the prowlers from seshego
the suspects that are always at large

*

boys from seshego, if you come again
i'm going to phafuri, the heartland of real sangomas
if you come here at ritruda number 12
you'll be trapped in my apartment
run around the house which will become an anthill
swarming bees & horseflies will sting your eyes & balls
you'll not collect my double-decker bed
you'll run around naked
dangling penises sweeping the floor
you'll bleat, slippery liquid forming in your mouths
you won't collect any red meat in the fridge
you won't take away my stove & toaster
your long fingers will be glued to my new plasma tv
boys from seshego, if you come again
end of the month, i'm going to phafuri
that heartland of real sangomas
if need be i'll even cross the limpopo
& mumithi river to lands yonder
sail to bileni, the land of makhayingi bila my great grandfather
i'll give the sangoma all my wages

we'll erect a fence of snakes to guard my house
against you, the boys from seshego
with your souls sucked out by vampires
with the shit job you've created for yourselves
whose only qualification is cruelty

Ancestral Wealth

For my father Risimati Daniel Bila: 1931-1989

I

Under these tall thorn umbrella trees
My ancestors dwell
Jonas is buried in a woven grass kenya
When Dayimani woke up dead at 10 am
He was buried in the afternoon, the same day
His body covered with white linen and a thin blanket
My ancestors dwell here
Seated, facing home in the east
Facing Bileni, far away in Mozambique
A broken mattress and xihlungwani *heaped on the grave*
Cracked enamel plates and mugs heaped on the grave

II

Papa, when you finally got admitted at Giyani Block
We thought the learned doctors who can see
What's hidden in blood and water
Would remove these needles
And pins and spears in your veins and wearied bones
But their bewitched green-red flashing machines in theatre
Confirmed you healthy
And when you got into the late night train to Garankuwa Hospital
Far away in Pretoria, on that ultra-distance bumpy ride
We thought the learned doctors
Would have removed this excruciating pain
In your chest and packing-up bones
But doctors in white gowns saw no fault in your stuttering engine
They sent you home
You got into that long bumpy train uncured
They asked you to come with your wife on 4th December 1989

For possible heart surgery
And the next day you came back home
Sat with your family around the fire
That night you didn't cough blood clots, nor groan
That night you didn't vomit
Nor was your body a river of sweat
Your face was sun-beaming
Blue eyes were shining
We ate chicken stew and pap
Drank Rooibos tea with buttered bread
That night owls and the wind didn't howl in trees
The mountain snake and dzelehani didn't cry
Dogs and cats didn't wail or mew
That night I slept like a baby

Under these tall thorn umbrella trees
My ancestors rise and hold hands
They sing in unison
Dance in rhythmic step
Around the fire

III

Wednesday 13 September 1989, 1 a.m.
You asked mother to extinguish the paraffin lamp
Burning on the red polished cement floor
The time to switch off your tormented heart beat had beckoned
That day you requested mhani N'wa-Noel
Your concubine from Mbhokota
To sleep in the grass-thatched rondavel with your girl children
Because the last night of intimacy
And pain belonged to your wife Fokisa N'wa-Mahatlani
Your black beauty of twenty six years
Yena wa ka mkhamu wa nsuku na ngwavila (She whose body glitters
with gold and gems)
Mbati ya ku fuma (The door to wealth)

29

Your last night belonged to your wife
Who birthed you seven healthy children
Children born between 1964 and 1980
The last night to outline your will –
Because you knew *n'wana wa munhu u le kusuhani*
The last night to outline how your homestead should be run
So that you don't return home wearing shorts
And run riot
In case your house was turned into a playground
Emachihweni, emathumbhanini
You sat on your three quarter bed
Wearing that brown striped t-shirt from Pep stores
Eyes fixed on the old leaking zinc roof
Then you paged through the Old Mutual policy document
And you said:
Mhana Oom   (he called me Oom)
Lwangu leri i ra khale   (The roof is old)
Switina ndzi xavile   (I have bought the bricks)
Kambe a swi nge eneli ku aka yindlu ya kahle   (But they'll not be
enough to build a decent house)
Loko va ku nyika swimalana swa mina swa phenxeni   (When they give
you my little pension fund)
Vumba yindlu   (Build a house)
*Kamara ya Oom, kamara ya Simon, kamara yin'wana ya Makhanani
na Julia*   (A room for Oom, a room for Simon, another room for
Makhanani and Julia)
Loko Xikwembu a xi lo ndzi nyika malembe ya nkombo yo hanya   (If
God had given me seven more years to live)
Oom na Simon a va ta va va ri ku tirheni   (Oom and Simon would be
working)
A va ta kota ku hlayisa Makhanani na Julia   (They would take care of
Makhanani and Julia)
Then the burning paraffin lamp was extinguished:
Each sleeping in their separate three quarter beds
Suddenly a heavy hand whipped mother's shoulder
It was her grandmother N'wa-Xakhombo

Whose voice shrieked:
Pfuka wena N'wa-Mafelalomo (Wake up, you who die in far distant places)
A wu swi voni leswaku wa weriwa? (Don't you see the roof is falling, collapsing upon you?)
All she heard was one groan
Hhmmm, hmmmm!
And papa, when she came to your three quarter bed
Daniel Risimati Bila the son of Dayimani and N'wa-Zulu
Had packed for good
Papa, your room was filled with cold air
Misty cloudy smog covered the room at 1 a.m.
Mama says you didn't hit or kick the walls violently
As you wrestled with the monster
Kwalaho ndzi n'wi longa (Then I laid out his body)
Ndzi koka minkumba ndzi zola milenge (I removed blankets and elevated his legs)
Ndzi lola mavoko ya longoloka na yena (I elevated his hands and arms along his body)
Ndzi vuyetela mahlo (I gently closed his eyes with a simple touch)
Ndzi n'wi sula xikandza (I wiped down his face)
A hlambile a nga se etlela (He had bathed before bedtime)
Mapfalo ya mina a ma file (I didn't feel any remorse)
Ivi ndzi khomelela mubedwa (Then I held the bed so firm)
Ndzi ku kumbe u ta pfuka (Thinking that he would wake up)
She searched for Rattex in the wardrobe
If she had found it
She would have crushed it
Swallowed it to burn her liver and heart
And join you in the other world
How would she raise her children
With cents from selling bananas and tomatoes
At the Elim market?

Under these tall thorn umbrella trees
My ancestors rise and hold hands

They sing in unison
Dance in rhythmic step
Around the fire

IV

'My time to go has arrived,' you told mother several times
The ZCC prophets Markos Mukhuva and *vho*-Ramantshwane
Had tearfully told you the same at Magangeni church:
Your life's ticket is over
They told you a few months before your departure
To the land yonder
They told you to stop chasing after the skirts
Because skirts were a cloth covering a big bottomless pit
And you came home to tell your wife
You were not taking anyone's cows nor calves in the kraal
But helping the wandering women in need
You lived facing the tomb
Facing the red setting sun
Knowing your living days
Were vanishing fast like paraffin paper fire
You lived facing the tomb
Knowing you couldn't afford skipping monthly subscriptions
To Saffas the undertaker in Louis Trichardt
Because the ancestors *emaxubini* were calling you
You lived facing the tomb
That's why you cleared the bushy shrubs
Making the road with a pick and shovel
Making the road with a spade and hoe
Because you wanted the hearse
To collect your remains at home with ease
Because you didn't want to be loaded in a wheelbarrow
And driven to be collected at the main road
Watched by birds, monkeys and stray dogs
You lived facing the tomb
Because papa, something so sharp was piercing you

Needles stinging your veins with deadly venom
Nails biting your flesh
The sharp spear jabbing your heart
Something so sharp was numbing your veins
Draining your energy from your bowels
You breathed heavily every time you climbed a steep hill
You coughed strenuously, sneezing, lungs rattled
Sometimes you collapsed on the narrow paths
After vomiting blood, groaning, vomiting air
Sometimes you bellowed
Like someone who had eaten fresh poison
But papa, you carried the burden of a family man
On your shoulders
Working every day of the week
Slowly walking ten kilometres every day
To Elim Hospital
For all these thirty years
Helping doctors carry out post-mortems –
Cutting through skulls, stitching and cleaning the dead so stinking
Burying the dead in black shrouds at ten o'clock every day
Behind the hospital sewerage
Papa, you did everything at Elim Hospital:
Ferrying patients to theatre
Feeding relieved mothers at the maternity wards
Scrubbing the floor in the Eye Department
Papa, you did everything at Elim Hospital
Just a for a paltry R300 salary in 1989
Because you had beaks to feed
Bodies to clothe

Under these tall thorn umbrella trees
My ancestors rise like elephants
At the break of dawn
To drink water
From the mountain's fountain

V

Saturday 26th September 1989 we hid you
In this sacred ground where shoes are taken off
It's not a cemetery for commoners
It's not Mazokhele nor Avalon
It's the Bila gardens, within my yard
It's a pity you spent two weeks in those mortuary pans
Ice must have burnt your skin and bones
Silencing the sense of hearing that never dies
Burning the growing beard and hair
When Saffas brought you home at dusk on Friday
In that dark hearse
Candles and a paraffin lamp burnt the whole night
In your lonely bedroom
The funeral parlour had bathed you
Dressed you in a white silky shroud
Mother and the elderly women wearing blankets
Slept on the floor around the coffin the whole night
In your two-roomed house
Papa, when you left us
Your three quarter bed was removed from the room
Put outside the house against the tree
I was a small boy of seventeen
Doing standard nine at Lemana High
For days I didn't go to school
Even though *a ka ha ri vusiku*
The elders said *ku fanele ku songiwa masangu*
I listened to *Ta lava hundzeke emisaveni* on Radio Tsonga
To hear your name mentioned on that dreadful programme
7am, your light brown casket covered with a blanket
Was displayed in the courtyard
We walked around it to view you for the last time
People cried, some fell to the ground so hard
It was the first time I saw a dead man
And the fallen man was my father

Who on that fateful night
Told mom that had he known better
That he would have died prematurely
He wouldn't have fathered his four last children
Including Oom
So I viewed you for the last time on earth
And I shed no tear because death had long come
I had seen you walk away
Eaten by an illness no doctor could detect

The night before the funeral
I sat around the big fire
Reverend Chabalala was preaching in the crowded tent
Papa, know that John Zulu your uncle donated a beast for the funeral
It was slaughtered *eka* Mapuve
80 kms away from Elim/Shirley
Papa, know that people spoke so well at your burial
Elias Machume was the Programme Director
Hahani N'wa-Risimati Xisana, in tears,
Informed the mourners about your death
And asked your ancestors Dayimani the son of Jonas
Jonas the son of Makhayingi
Makhayingi *wa* Mpfumari
Mpfumari *wa* Xanjhinghu
Xanjhinghu *wa* Ntshovi
Ntshovi *wa* Xisilafole *xi nga ri na nhonga xi sila hi mandla*
To receive you on the other side
Your brother John Bila who had disappeared
for more than twenty years
Came back home the day you died
He trembled, speaking on behalf of the family
Can't remember what he said, because he said nothing, but cried
Your wife's brother J. S. Mashele also paid tribute to you
Even your colleagues from Elim Hospital came in numbers
They sang hymns melodically
P. Mathavha spoke on behalf of the ZCC

Meriam Shetlele represented the neighbourhood
Thomas Mahlasela read the wreaths
Sivara Rev Maluleke the short and handsome friend of yours
And carried your coffin to the grave
The ZCC *mokhukhu* men danced in khaki and *manyanyatha*
Chonaphi Cawuke, Phineas N'wavungavunga, Shilowa,
Mahanci and Xikhudu the great dancers were there
The yard was full of mourners
Men wearing jackets and women draped in blankets
Even The Lion of Judah, your first wife's brother, was there!
He gave the vote of thanks with his moving coarse voice
Mourners contributed cash –
It was recorded in a book. It was good money.
But some members of my family with long fingers
Never showed all the money to my mother
I was still small papa but I've forgiven these thieves
We planted your remains
Filled the grave with blood red soil
It had a hump like a bull
The elderly planted maize, beans, corn and pumpkins
Inviting the rain to come
Because your death was never going to bring famine
And starvation in this house
The elderly placed coins and your preferred drinking mug and plate
On the grave
We laid you beside your mother Makhanani N'wa-Zulu
Who died on 16 November 1980
And your father Dayimani who died in June 1964
A white cross marked your name:
Daniel Risimati Bila
Rest in peace

Under these tall thorn umbrella trees
My ancestors rise and hold hands
They sing in unison
Dance in rhythmic step
Around the fire

VI

Papa, you came home to rest forever
Because Giyani Block breeds the pungent death smell
Shallow breathing skeletons crumble in the crowded ward
With no family member to preserve their sanity
The jaws lock, eyes fixed
And the white pupils enlarged in the light so bright

Papa, you came home to rest forever
Because shivering patients with bluish lips
Watch tearfully as the final air bursts from the belly
Of a patient next door, bursting like a detonated bomb
Misty air blackening the ward with coldness

The restless patients with irregular pulse
Watch helplessly as the nurses remove the linen
With that stinking last black stool
Transferring this man who died in the night to another ward –
Next to a living patient in a single room
The living patient is happy he's got a neighbour
But the neighbour is fast asleep, wearing a shroud
The new neighbour is neither hungry nor thirsty
The living starts to hallucinate
Gets lost in nappies
Now he knows the nurses brought him a strange ghost
Who'll gnaw at his dreams

Papa, you came home to rest forever
Because in this hospital, like many hospitals
Just an hour after someone has been confirmed dead by the doctor
The nurses make up the same bed
A new patient sleeps in there comfortably
He doesn't know someone has just died there
He collects the spirit of the dead
In the middle of the night

The new patient rushes to the toilet to pray
Pleading to see his only son from Joburg
And when his son arrives the next morning
And holds his father's cold hand
The old man opens his mouth with difficulty
As if to say, my son take care of my cattle
But no word shoots from the mouth layered with white foam
And again goes another patient
In broad daylight

Papa, you came home to rest forever
Because the groaning and wailing movie never stops in the hospital
Some pale-faced patients urinate in coffee mugs and plates
The very same mugs they use for coffee and tea
Some patients jump from the bed like impalas
Tearing drips and tubes away
They race around the ward wearing the catheters
Bubbling with urine tea
They too scream in hallucination:
Nurse, come and help
They are here with knives
They want to suffocate me
They want to cut my throat

In the intensive care unit, someone is motionless
Trapped in a truncation
His car rolled three times into the donga
His head was almost crushed
Perhaps he's brain dead
But the heart is still beating slowly
The nurses feed him
They change his nappies every hour
His family won't allow the medics to
Switch off the life support machine
Because though he's brain dead
Miracles can still happen

They happened in the days of Jesus Christ
And when his spear suddenly rises
The nurses know the brain dead patient's life ticket is still intact

Some burnt-out nurses simply talk on cellphones
Watching this ongoing groaning and vomiting and shitting drama
But you papa, you didn't want to die in hospital
like your mother Makhanani N'wa-Zulu
Who spent five months at Shangaan Block without eating
Nor going to the toilet on her own
My grandmother who died alone
Who when her coffin was opened for viewing
Even a brave man like you Papa, cried
Because there was no one to close her mouth

Papa, you came home to rest forever
Like Dayimani your father
And Jonas your grandfather
And Makhayingi your great grandfather
You came home to rest forever
After a family meal
In the hands of your wife
In your bed
In the morning so still

VII

If you were alive today, madala –
I'd buy you a suit and soft skin ostrich shoes
I'd fly you to Durban or Cape Town
So you can walk on the beach
Feel the soft grains of summer sand
I'd take you out to sit-down restaurants
Try out shrimps, mussels and this good food I eat

If you were alive today, madala –

We would plant avocado and litchi trees
Grow spinach and beetroot together
Pinch and prune sweetest tomatoes that yield
You would teach me how to dig a trench
How to prepare a seedbed for seedlings
How to make ridges and furrows
How to mulch and make compost and manure
How to save water and use grey water
We would grow those red roses
And maintain those white lilies
We would do gardening on our ancestral land
Singing your song:
7/8 u ya lithanda isaka la mazambani
U ya lithanda isaka la mazambani

If you were alive today, madala –
You would tell me how you survived the white dog
That followed you every morning to work
The dog that would run fast past you
The strange dog that would slide through your legs
Or even hit your legs with its tail
The dog that walked ahead of you
The dog that numbed your feet
The dog that shook and wearied your bones
The dog that disappeared at the bus stop
Just before the hospital gate
The same white *vaveni* that received you back from work
But couldn't enter the gate to your house
To throw you into a grave

If you were alive today, madala –
You would tell me about that rope
That roamed in your nightmares
The rope that made you so impatient
That made you hate everything about your wife
The rope that made you hit her

And want to kill her with a knife
The rope of which prophet Muvhangeli said:
U nga yi rhwaleli loko u yi vona endleleni ya wena   (Don't pick it up
when you find it placed on your path)
The tough rope of wicked relatives
Who had long sized your neck

If you were alive today, madala –
You would tell me how you and Ngholeni picked up that dead rabbit
Early in the morning on your way to work
How you skinned the rabbit with delight
How you wanted to cook it for lunch
When suddenly a strange man came
And touched your forehead
And said, *"and hi yena papantsongo wa Frank."*
Then your forehead ached and pounded
And when you came back home from work
The same strange man
Hobbled to your house
All he said was one sentence:
I needed to find Frank's brother's place
Then he vanished
Stealing your heart
Placing it in a cave
Planting a cockerel's heart in you
And you coughed and coughed

VIII

Papa, I know it took us twenty years to erect your tombstone
All along the wind was blowing you away
The sun was burning you
Your pillow was your hand
But now Bila, Mhlahlandlela, rest in peace
Do not open the grave and come home wearing shorts
Since you left, your wife has remained in the house

I've not seen a man sitting on your chair
It's still your house
Full of trees and vegetables

7/8 u ya lithanda isaka la mazambani
U ya lithanda isaka la mazambani

Missing

For my cousin-brothers Daniel Makhubele and Joel Hon'wana

we are still searching for you
even under water
in the passing of flies
sangomas have thrown the bones & shells
calling upon you to take the road
to Elim or Louis Trichardt or Giyani
even if it means collecting a tree branch & soil pigments
to lay your souls in peace at home
we are ready to do so
but still, when the clouds form
& the swallows soar above the sky
there is no thunder
no letter, no call from Botswana
when the clouds gather
& the swallows soar above the sky
no letter, no call from Johannesburg
we await knocks at the door
your presence has fumed into shades & shadows
yet you dwell in our dreams
you still shine sprightly even in the sun
travellers & prophets say you are still alive
but it's been years waiting now
we pray you've not been devoured
by eagles & jackals
we pray you've not been crushed by rocks
deep in the belly of the earth

another year goes by
the sun goes down
the moon comes up

trains and taxis that deliver migrant workers home
still have no room for you
my brother Joel Hon'wana
mhani Patironi Langisa N'wa-Mahatlani Maxele
wants to cuddle her grandchild
since you left Bungeni village in the '90s
for factories or who knows what ...
in Mjipa *emavonini*
your trousers and shirts
still hang neatly in the wardrobe

another year goes by
the sun goes down
the sun comes up

buses and wagons that ferry *magayisa* home
still miss you
my brother Daniel Mangundu Makhubele
mhani Dayina N'wa-Mahatlani Maxele
wants to hug her great grandchild
since you left Chavani village in July 1978
after the death of your grandfather Mahatlani Maxele
for the mines somewhere in Brits
or Rustenburg

your mirror is the soundless gramophone and vinyls
you left behind
the N'wa-Xinyamani girl you wanted to marry
imagined you in the moonlight
under the twilight sky of the red setting sun
in your absence
her blood rushed to the head
she found Mzamani next door
she knew waiting for you

44

sweet handsome dude in suit
equalled waiting for the moon

another year goes by
the sun goes down
the moon comes up

if you had left behind a girl
perhaps she would fetch granny some water
if you had left a boy
perhaps he would chase the birds
& locusts plundering the mealie fields
now that she's old & slow
someone would be making *mukapu*
wash her beaded *salempore* wraps
& sweep the yard

another year goes by
the sun goes down
the sun comes up

feeble *baba* Ceneka waits helplessly
in the smothering zinc house
can't walk to wash at Ritavi river anymore
it's 30 years since he's been like that
knocked down by a stroke when you left
even when your nose smells the fragrance
of figs and wild berries
still, can't you remember
nkuwa wa le kaya eMaphanyini
xifuva xaku xi file xana?

another year goes by
the sun goes down
the moon comes up

your mother's face is a turbulent ocean
heavy dry tears drip in her long nights
her heart is weighed down
by the burdens of birth
apostolic prophets she's consulted
she's splashed *xiwacha* in the yard
& across the field
to chase away dragons
mountaineering on your back
prophets say you are still alive
somewhere in Botswana
married to a Motswana
& perhaps you still work in the mines

another year goes by
the sun goes down
the sun comes up

the man who claims to know your whereabouts says
if we come to look for you
in far-away lands
we should not ask for Daniel Makhubele
because now you are Lion Makhubele
the man who claims to know your whereabouts
says your in-laws want to meet *baba* Ceneka and *mhani* Dayina
but you say your parents have silently left this world
yes, beloved N'wa-Sewula your grandmother
died in her sleep at Vuk' zenzele
in your absence

& when you come back
go to her grave
sprinkle some snuff
splash *mqomboti*
ses' Emily is back home
exhausted by menial work on ZZ2 farms
whacked away by stroke
this year her daughter Nqobile
died on granny's back

another year goes by
the sun goes down
the moon comes up

elder brother – handsome dude
what dreams wander in your sleep
when we are anguished & pained like this?
mhani Dayina lives in prayer
she's a pensioner
old & slow
she takes care of bed-ridden *baba* Ceneka

another year goes by
the sun goes down
the sun comes up

will you still find the zigzagging path
to Maphanyini and Manyunyu
or are we chasing an elusive dream
while your fats are burning
to extend some witch's days on earth forever?
elders say *gungu ra tirha*

valoyi va pfurhetela
leswaku mi nga voni ndlela ya le kaya
ancestors, God, please have mercy
wipe the trachoma from the eyes of your lost children

another year goes by
the sun goes down
the sun comes up

my brother Daniel, my brother Joel, come home!
we eat fresh pap & tasty chicken
gobble down jelly & custard
we crush crispy bread
sip tea & coffee
we dress in lavish wear
to celebrate Christmas
but there's no grain in your bowls
the whirlwind howls in your mugs
your seats around the table are vacant
maybe where you are it is raining & cold
your toes wet without shoes
perhaps you start daily rounds
as dry-lipped toothless beggars
who sleep under bridges
in plastic & card box
hit by nervous breakdown
each year we slaughter a goat
& munch *swoswo*
to celebrate New Year
perhaps you squander time in drinking holes
with toothless over-sexed whores
perhaps what you eat is *murahela-kule*
are you victims of *mencwa*
with fractured bones
& germane & prescient minds deranged?

another year goes by
the sun goes down
the moon comes up

elders say
in every household there's the worst case
my mothers carry heavy hearts
they weep angrily
i am born of the same womb
the womb that breeds men
who walk in the weeds
and when Kenyan thugs detained me
at Jomo Kenyatta Airport
on my visit to the World Social Forum
in January 2007
they said:
"your passport is mutilated
not even a Kenyan can be allowed
to pass through customs with this ragged passport."
i prayed in silence
God help me
don't keep me in this dungeon for good
my fiancée is pregnant with young Vonani Bila
i don't want to follow in the path of my brothers
those who miss the road to Elim
even in broad daylight

perhaps if we had firms & mines in Bungeni–
our hearts wouldn't be aching so
perhaps if we had a tarred road
hotels and airports in Chavani –
we would be riding in your cars
perhaps one day we angered you so much
that's why you packed your bags…
perhaps you are no longer yourselves

but zombies
or maybe you've used the rope to meet your gods
or a truck has hit you dead-flat
now your spirits wander
in the accident-prone roads.

we shall not burn your dust-gathering suits
nor throw away the shoes you left polished
your trunk tins are still full of *things*
& perhaps photographs of girls you wished to marry
we shall not burn your vests,
underwear & socks
please come home
even if you are accompanied
by surrogate wives
your moms' age
please come home
we'll send you to *muti* headquarters Phafuri
or drive you to zion city Moria
to exorcize the *mencwa* chemistry
mi fanele ku biwa hi ximoko
mi fembiwa
mi rhadzunuriwa
leswaku swifuva swi ta pfuleka.

a year goes by
the sun goes down
the sun comes up

Autobiography

Thanks Nazim Hikmet

I

I was born in 1972
Where Mudzwiriti River swelled over roads and boulders
But nothing green grew in Gazankulu Bantustan
Even plants and trees and shrubs
Even the animals and birds and reptiles
Even the mountains and lakes and streams
Felt the pain of apartheid war
I still live here in the backwoods
With the common people
Warming ourselves around bonfires

I've slept in grand sky-scraping hotels
And villas of the world's jaw-dropping cities –
My name is inscribed in books, postcards, newspapers, zines and films
But I've never been active on Facebook or Twitter
When I finally sleep
I want to be folded neatly
Planted into a family cemetery
Head facing east
Please my children, don't pile up goods on the grave
The rain will wash my memory away
The sun will dry them and wild fire will burn me to ashes
Please my children, don't be foolish and chop the trees
I planted with passion
They're your future oxygen, bread and soup

Though I possess no clattering wheel
Or a bike spoke and chain
I've lived like a swallow –
Weaving nests across the mountains and oceans

I've ridden in rickshas, buses, trains, planes and dilapidated taxis
In boats, motorbikes and donkey carts
I've been chauffeured in bombastic cars
To attend meetings with ministers,
Social movements, artists, culture gurus, donors, NGOs and professors
The woman at the Polokwane Airport check-in counter
Feels pity for my wife in the village as I fly out to cities on Fridays

I grew up in a mud hut
Drank water from the wells
Slept on the itchy *majekejeke* mat on a cowdung-smeared floor
At 10, I was still wetting myself in the night
The millipede powder couldn't stop the habit either
I showered from a plastic basin
Often used a water-filled mug to wipe my face
And extinguished the rotten rat wreaking havoc in my armpits
But I've also lived in an apartment with portraits
And tidy rooms for visitors
And yes, I've also lived in an apartment with racing roaches
And wet laundry

I grew up using a long-drop toilet
Newspaper, *mugabagaba* and guava tree leaves wiping my backside
Others used stones and bare hands to clean themselves in the bush
Later I enjoyed steam baths and massage in spas
Sat in armchairs, rode a horse and walked on red carpets
One day I may receive a Nobel Prize for Literature
Like Neruda, Brodsky and Szymborska

At 25, I danced in a sunlit pool almost naked
I sat in a Stockholm public sauna with staggering old white couples
Watching me cuddling my Camilla who wept like a baby
Because her black man couldn't relocate to first world
Under apartheid, it was immoral to kiss a white woman

At 35, I spent three hours at Jomo Kenyatta airport jail

For travelling on a valid yet tattered passport
I met a Chinese, an Ethiopian and a Somalian
Who had been there for three months
Prison warders forced them to agree
That they were Al Qaeda operatives
Trained in the caves and mountains of Afghanistan or Pakistan
That they knew where the bearded Osama bin Laden was hiding

We sat on linen-free bunks, tortured by anopheles mosquito parasites
We were fed spinach and rice in a plastic
With no plate or spoon to eat with
I didn't have dollars to bribe Mulongo my captor
With mocking disdain
I prayed frantically:
God, Gudani my girlfriend is pregnant
A human heart is beating in her womb
It's my first child
Six years later, I watch fire swelling into flames
Jomo Kenyatta Airport gutted by a deafening inferno
Airport banks charred; flights redirected
I see officers passing water buckets in attempts to quash the blaze
But Kenya is a country without fire engines
Six years ago, I was detained there
Though I know nothing about the Taliban or al Qaeda or Boko Haram

I return to my birthplace gawking at the forming clouds
But Shirley village is a dark shadow –
Foul witchcraft air floats at midnight
Woolly dogs gather on my stoep and bark and wail
Strange cats mew outside my window
Owls hoot over the water tank, the wind howls in reply
Madzelehani – Bush babies – yell like infants in the avocado trees

Though I love the smell of rain, I fear when thunder rumbles
Lightning shakes the big oak tree that's been there for years
At forty, the prophet in Moria told me some people are jealous

They want me to go round the bend, family in disarray
But even when my eyes are shut at night, they won't succeed

I stash holy salt granules in pockets when I walk
Sprinkle ZCC spring water on my face and in the house
To scare off the barking dogs that want to maul me
Here, I fear to walk on *xifula* planted in the yard
Or drink from a *xidyisa*-spiked cup at a party or funeral
Ndzi chava ku pepejeriwa ndzi duga naro ku fana na tatana   (I'm scared
to be sent away to the wilderness of madness like dad)
Ndzi chava ku nusiwa nkondzo hi valoyi va tiko leri   (I'm scared to be
bewitched by witches of this land)
Va nyankhandli xiyani wa ngove si nga fi!   (The cruel witches who
only deserve to perish)
That's why at bedtime I put the Bible under the pillow
But I was never scared of the Boers and their dogs

I return to my birthplace gawking at the forming clouds
But the unyielding comrades in power know all about tenders,
Cars, villas, soapies, sushi parties and holidays –
In fact they are a set of carnivores
Lethal tigers, leopards and lions
They are adult *izikhothane* –
The type that burn banknotes and new clothes when stoned
Look, they own krugerrands and gold bars
Live in marble houses with servants
Drink from gilded cups
They entertain guests with pipe and beer
Yet expect us the voters to drink urine
And wash our faces with sweat and saliva

Don't they see the impassable roads and mud in my toes?
Don't their hearts bleed when we push coffins in wheelbarrows,
In the pelting rain to bury the dead?
Are they not haunted by sun-bleached children
Shuffling sand on foot to catch education

in indescribable broken down schools?

Here, meek souls live in gloomy mud huts
Silhouetted with sparkles of fireflies
Moonlit streets with intermittent electricity
Though I served as a guerrilla against the apartheiders
I still walk on the scorching gravel roads

II

Mama says her pregnancy was a nightmare
A horde of witches were pointed by papa
N'wa-Mahatlani had to chew boiled roots of kweek grass
To keep me growing in the war-zone womb

At three months mama went to Dombani
The village foreign veterinarian
The hefty vet who had drugs for horses, cats, dogs and bulls asked:
U twa yini? U huma kwihi?   (What's your problem? Where do you
come from?)
Ndzi huma eka Mr Phillips.   (I come from Mr Phillips)
Why u nga yanga eka Phillips?   (Why didn't you go to Mr Phillips?)
Hikuva mirhi ya wena yi strong dokodela.   (Because your medicine is
much stronger, doctor!)
Perhaps that's why I didn't leave the womb wounded
But the womb-war persisted:
At five months, Jacques the limping Swiss doctor at Elim Hospital
Put a torch-like gadget deep in mama's womb
It sucked all the unwanted blood
Mama was haemorrhaging before birth time

Head up, legs down
Chonaphi the ZCC fellow advised mama to drink *mogabolo*
So when she got to the maternity ward
She didn't have to incessantly hit the walls in agony
A minute was enough to throw me out unharmed, without pain

I'd criss-crossed and jived in the womb for ten months
Tuesday 1972, 8pm, fresh and strong I emerged
Yet with a tiny frame
There was no nurse or doctor to help with delivery
I swam through like a fish
Mommy wondered why she had to take me home
Instead of keeping her bundle in a bottle
The Swiss doctor nicknamed Mushathama said:
Vona n'wana wa wena wa tika   (Your child is weighty)
U na rhambu ro tiya   (He has a strong bone)
A nga fani na lava nga tala khuvi   (Unlike those fatty-foam children)
A nga vabyi, u fresh   (He's not sick, he's fresh)

III

When I was three, the sun had just set
When I set alight mama's grass-thatched windowless hut
She was busy cooking on an open fire
The sky was dark covered by black smog
The fire consumed all her bracelets, the bangles, *minceka, swibelana* ...
All the adornments that made her young
Burnt to ashes, burnt to ashes
I ran to the neighbours for shelter because none could fight that fire
Scared to be whipped

The next day mama took me to Xidonkana the prophet at Mbhokota
I had to be exorcised, demons had to be chased away
The dreadlocked prophet kept me in a stone hut he had built
In his New Jerusalem up in the hill
The singing women of the Apostolic church
Quickly covered the hut with old blankets
And thick construction red and green plastic
I burnt in the sauna

His disciples brought red burning stones
Poured them in the bucket

I burnt, I burnt
They added a bucket of hot water
Mixed with a bowl of coarse salt granules
They asked me to inhale the vapours without flinching
I burnt, I burnt
Cow-hide drums were throbbing outside the stone hut
Goatee-bearded Jackson Xidonkana Hlungwani
Stood outside by the makeshift door barefoot
His dreadlocks dangling over his white gown and red crosses
He turned and twirled a carved stick and burst into song:
Yesu, Hosi ya vhangeli   (Jesus, Lord of evangelists)
Tanani mi ta horisa timbilu   (Come, set your hearts free)
Na swifula mi ta susa   (Come and cure your cancers)
… tatani mi ta horisa timbilu   (Come and set your hearts free)
Na swidyisa mi ta susa   *(*Come and rid yourselves of the toxins)
… tanani mi ta horisa timbilu   *(*Come, set your hearts free)
Na swinkhovha mi ta susa   (And the owls will be tamed)
… tanani mi ta horisa timbilu   (Come, set your hearts free)
Na tinyoka mi ta susa   (And the snakes will be removed)

The *mafufunyani* felt the heat
And escaped in haste
Like tokoloshi dashing to the river
Xidonkana asked me and mom to drink and wash with steamed water
He called the red dirty water the blood of Jesus

       IV

At 7, me and my brothers had come back from school
It was time to release the goats to graze
Tlhoko! Tlhoko!   (There it's a bird's nest)
I dyinyenyani   (It's a big bird)
Up in an umbrella thorn tree a child lay in a nest

She smiled, bent down like someone praying
We stood there motionless, helpless

She had a furrowed forehead and a pointed nose
Her tiny fingers tightly held the nest
We raced home and reported this strange thing we saw

My father, the only ZCC priest in the village, prayed for us
Stroked every part of our bodies with *kotana*
Then we burnt in the sauna
The next day the baby and the nest were gone
But no grave had opened at home

V

At 11, papa sent me to Elim Hospital for circumcision
That's where Herbert Stanley Phillips the son of a missionary
Had taken him at the same age
Kokwani John Xihosana Zulu wanted me to sing *hogo* in the mountain
Sit with my back around the undying fire
Sleep in a nest like a bird
Drink *malusu* to forget my warm blankets at home
And my mother's hot meals
Kokwani John Zulu wanted me to watch *vadzabi* carry logs at dawn,
And make fire.
He wanted me to wear red ochre and wield sticks of triumph
He wanted me to learn *milawu* and chants by heart
Learn to eat *xivonelo* with hands tied at the back
Survive sharp blades or just wither and die
He wanted me to wear a warrior name like Khazamula,
Khanghela, Xitlhangoma,
Risimati, Hlengani, Yingwani, Hasani, Magigwani
Maduvula, Mphahlele, Mzamani, Mhlava, Mahatlani
Mafemani, Magezi, Mandlakazi, Gaza, Gezani, Skheto,
I'm happy I didn't go to the camps shrouded in mystery
Where boys are told to stop living until *madlala* expires
Where boys must look down and not face the burning fire
For fear of death
I'm happy I didn't go to the circumcision camps shrouded in mystery

Where villagers must stop ploughing or digging
Or listening to the radio
Or playing music out loud

For a month or weeks beds must not shake
All we do is to sing one song *hogo huwelela*
And celebrate when boys keep away from water for days
Just to horde ticks in the name of culture
But a certain chief simply collects cash to enrich himself
Instead of building roads, paving streets, schools,
Clinics for his forgotten people

I'm happy I didn't go to expose my tiny frame
To that cold weather in the bush camps
Where scores of dehydrated boys died
In Mpumalanga's botched circumcision camps
Boys bled to death
Some only come back with gangrene and amputated manhood
Denied drinking water and nourishing food
I think of my two boys...
Oh no, I won't send them there
What type of a father would send his boys
To suffer in the extreme cold, suffer malnutrition?

I became a man at Elim Hospital in view of nurses
I was too young to admire their breasts
They pierced me with an injection
And the part they pierced died for a while
Then they pulled my foreskin over the head of my short penis
They did that with a pair of forceps
My foreskin was snipped by female nurses
They stitched the wound
And dressed it with a bandage
They gave me pain killers
But I walked home like a crab
They told me not to sit around the fire

Or ride bicycles, *swigirigiri* and *swibantsheke*
I was too young to have sex or masturbate with my bandage on
Papa insisted that I use Vaseline to get the wound to heal faster
After a week, I removed the bandage and I was a man
I saw the stitches falling off like weathered feathers
Now I can speak at board meetings and chief's kraal boldly
Knowing that I've the required arsenal against Aids

At 13, I called myself Vonani –
Because I admired Vonani the sassy taxi driver from Mbhokota
But village pals call me Tete the savvy dancer
At three I used to sing and dance
Tete hi tee, Tete hi tee!
Tete hi tee, Tete hi tee!
Corn-beer drinkers would beat enamel paint tins and clap
Singing along *Tete hi tee!*

Some children wear names of monsters
Hitler, Idi Amin, Cecil Rhodes, Mugabe, Dlayani, Matlakala
I wear my grandfather's name Dayimani –
The man who walked to Kimberley
The man who dug diamond in the big gaping hole
The man who came home with a truck full of suits,
Bags of corn and sugar
To feed the Makhayingi Bila clan of hunters
But there wasn't a single shining diamond in the bags

I wanted to call myself Mkhacani, Dayimani's other name
But Mkhacani means to urinate
Villagers who love me call me *Dayimani ya Maphutukezi na Manghezi*
Every time Albert Jesi meets me, he sings:
Ndzi tsakile ngopfu ndzi nga vuya na dayimani (I'm delighted I've
brought home diamond)
Ndzi nga vuya na dayimani (I've brought home diamond)

VI

At 12 I went to Shirley Presbyterian church for the whole year
I didn't know I was wasting my energy and time
With these Bible lessons
End of the year, 22 December 1985 in church –
The elders of the church and their reverend E F C Mashava
Wielded a Samurai sword
To behead the son of a peasant:
He asked the son of a peasant Freddy Vonani Bila
And three others to stand before the congregation
While other children were receiving their certificates of katekisma
I shivered as the elders with flowing garbs mocked us:
Your parents are members of that ZCC church that crushes steel
They walk around with a shining metal star
They worship a mere mortal when they should be worshipping Jesus
We cannot baptize you, because you are still minors
I returned home with a heavy heart
Mama cried bitterly, tears beneath her eyes
I had never seen her weep before
When she saw mud on my face
I had been told that without a baptism certificate
The Boers wouldn't give me a job
In their Christian South Africa
Since 1985, I've never set foot in that church
I can't listen to sermons of the intoxicated
Who collide with witches in the dark
The mud they threw on my face couldn't stick
I silently put colonial doctrine on the floor

1986, I read Karl Marx's *Capital*
and *The Communist Manifesto* at Akanani
Hambileswi a yo na yi xa (Even though it rained and cleared)
It was better than wailing in churches, temples, synagogues
Or consulting sangomas and prophets
Which is what most people do

At Akanani, there were whites from Joburg, Durban and Cape Town
They liked to greet people
Gave us lifts from Shirley to Elim or Louis Trichardt
Or Polokwane or Johannesburg
They played football with the common folk
Some learnt to speak Xitsonga and Tshivenda fluently
Mike and Astrid sent their child Cabral to a village school
They wore red-shirts with messages of revolution and faded jeans
Since meeting them in the night political school
I've read Marx, Lenin, Gramsci, Freire, Boal, Gaddafi
Nyerere, Cabral, Sankara, Fanon, Ernest Mandel
They taught me how to run a co-operative
How to use theatre to get people to talk
About their daily problems like lack of water

We travelled around the province doing theatre for development
I knew, "unless we organize, we'll be washed away!"
Eighteen years into liberation
I still question those who are not fit to govern
Those who loot in the name of the struggle
I'm glad this government won't hang me
For speaking frankly, not yet anyway

At 18, I distributed *samizdat* pamphlets
And recited poems in ANC rallies
In Thohoyandou, Makwarela, Vleifontein, University of the North
We organized consumer boycotts
Against the white shops in Louis Trichardt
But now the white shops are in Elim
Alongside spaza shops of the Pakistani, Nigerians and Somalians
My rural folk remain beggars on their land
Talk of black economic empowerment is empty
Comrades who shouted long live Marx and Lenin
And Lumumba and Sankara
Don't have a socialist vision
They build a billion-rand Gautrain that doesn't go to Soweto

Or Mamelodi where people live
Yet expect a vote from the stranded, desperate township folk
I live not too far from Muyexe
Where millions are being wasted by tenderpreneurs
I dream of a speed train from Elim to Cape Town
I dream of a university in my village
I dream of tarmac roads to replace zigzagging village paths
I dream of public parks and sports facilities
I don't want to live in the world of butchers of miners
When my father died, I got my passport in Sibasa
I wanted to cross the Limpopo river and join MK in Lusaka
Return home like *inyamazane* with an AK47 over my shoulders
Singing gloriously over a hippo for freedom:
Sabasiya abazali emakaya   (We've left our parents at home)
Siwela emazweni   (Fleeing to lands far away)

The dream evaporated, exiles were returning home
At Codesa, Mandela and De Klerk were smoking the same pipe
But I joined the MK defence unit at Akanani
Received a crash course on arms and guerrilla warfare
I never fought in a battle. Wouldn't like to spill blood.
But my dance is toyi toyi:
Kubi kubi kubi   (Although things are bad)
Siyaya, siyaya, siyaya ePitoli   (But we are going to Pretoria)
Noma basishaya   (Even when they beat us)
Siyaya, siyaya, siyaya ePitoli   (We are going to Pretoria)
Noma basidubula   (Even when they shoot us)
Siyaya, siyaya, siyaya ePitoli   (We are going to Pretoria)

But when I walk on gravel and count bodies decomposing
Patients sleeping on the floor and benches
Patients who will not be sent to x-ray because there's no money
Or the machine is broken
Black patients who don't matter in the eyes of a black government
I feel like bombing Luthuli House
Burning down parliament like the Burkinabe masses chasing away

Their president the dictator
But it won't happen, I can't bomb my comrades.
I am a man of peace, I hate to spill blood.

VII

At 14, I went to Lemana High in Magangeni
Eduardo Mondlane had sat at the same desk
Today that school that taught the community
To grow their own vegetables
Build their houses and make their tables and chairs
Is overgrown by vegetation and weeds
I hated the separate staff rooms for black and white teachers
But I enjoyed inter-school sport and eisteddfod
I walked 14 kms on foot everyday
Because Majeje the homeland puppet
Couldn't build a high school in my village
It was good to be taught by good teachers
But some white teachers taught us with contempt and disdain
While lazy black teachers cared only for cash, girls and beer
I hated teachers who dragged their sorrows and egos to the classroom
Instead of teaching with passion

At 17, my father died
I still don't know what killed him
I have no photo frame to hang on the wall
Ms Jacobs my Afrikaans teacher with a heart comforted me
It felt like she would adopt me
Perhaps the black boy from the village was going to work
In the garden, earn some income
Sit silently around the table and eat *potjiekos*, tomato *bredie*
And mutton stew with rice
Perhaps the black boy was going to enjoy the taste
Of biltong and *dröewors*
I shrugged, not me; there's peace in my mother's windowless mud hut

I couldn't dodge lessons at Lemana
I smiled every time I saw Nyeleti's oval face
I wanted to hear the tenderness of her baritone voice
Touch her pushback hair style
When she wasn't in class, my day was wasted
Inside I was burning, but poverty shut my lips with a padlock
Nyeleti is the reason I completed matric
There must be valid reasons to go to school
But Nyeleti kept me alive
Not a degree, or big house or car in the future
But her glistening smile

VIII

At 19 I went to Tivumbeni College of Education
It wasn't my intention to be a pedagogue
I wanted to be a ceramicist or journalist
I've always admired brave journalists
Nosy and sniffing
But everyone who ate bread and cheese, bacon and eggs
In the village was a teacher, nurse or railway worker
I completed my teacher's diploma with three distinctions
But never worked as a teacher

At 19, Ntsan'wisi closed the college for the whole year
Angry students loaded Hager the rector on the back of the bakkie
I hated *Spesiaal Afrikaans* with passion
I was at college to study Economics
What was special about Afrikaans
When children were mowed down in Soweto 76?

At 22, people voted in Mandela's men and women to power
It was good to see long queues of hope
My hope was elevated when former unionists went to parliament
I imagined a new country without sprawling shacks
Though I supported the Reconstruction and Development Programme

I didn't vote for Joe Slovo's sunset clause
I supported Azapo, but this party of Biko will never win the elections
When the RDP was suspended, and replaced by Gear
I faxed a poem to President Mandela's office
Mandela, Have You Ever Wondered?
... that the triumphant crowd retires to ghettos?

At 20, I had sex for the first time
It was late at night, in a dark room at Tivumbeni College
With a high school girl
Khosa my friend took me there. He had made the arrangement.
The girl had come to see the college with her school
I don't remember her name
I wouldn't remember her even if we meet in Bushbuckridge
The teacher vulture didn't use any condom
I didn't have one, and I wouldn't have known how to use it
If she fell pregnant; then I'm sorry my dear girl
My seeds fell on the rocks

In my first year at Tivumbeni I shared a room with boys from Valdezia
They drank every week, they drank everything
Used hungry girls from Nkowankowa like dogs before my eyes
Girls camped in the room from Friday to Monday morning
Groaning all night long; groaning all day long
Sometimes these boys would growl and bleed,
Complaining of drop and gonorrhoea
I wouldn't catch anything like that
Would you get drunk and hurt from watching a porno?

IX

I treasure the women I loved
But my one night stands were a disaster
Lele, svelte with big eyes, used to drink wine at my flat in Pregrado
When she was drunk we would kiss
Feel my hard stick rubbing her thighs

One morning she came over
She was on her way to Joburg
I drank body-boosting *mageu* but the dick was lame
So I ashamedly let her go, catch a taxi to Joburg
Years later, I met her, she was frail and weak
She'd lost hair and weight
I'm glad *mageu* didn't give my body any boost that morning
I thought of the days she used to be driven in BMWs
Charmza baby in expensive sunglasses and labels

My one night stands were a disaster
With Prim, that girl who loved every man with bling bling
My stick was hard, but the traffic light was red
She was drunk from her red wine
At the Cape Town Hollow hotel she shouted in her coconut tone:
"Don't be a typical Xhosa man,
My white guy doesn't mind licking me
It's sweet with blood, flowing blood."
I chose to be a typical Xhosa man
Who is scared to cough blood clots
Scared to shit droppings like a goat
Scared that my system might be blocked
For I want to crawl, live until hundred years
Where I come from they say *swa yila wa yila*

I wish I were like King Solomon
The poet with 700 wives and 300 concubines
But I'm far from matching his record
I picked up a wandering town girl one night
She followed me to the Glenkens apartment at Hans van Rensburg
We had a Nando's grilled chicken, pap and a Coke for supper
She slept with her tight jeans on
Until morning
Can't remember her name
Nor where she came from
She was a girl with a sweet voice

She wasn't a ghost.
No, I can't remember her
It doesn't bother me either
Her unshaved armpits were *meerkat* smelling
She was *mushavhanamadi* – a spider in the web
Or should I say a croc that lives in water but refuses to wash
I slept looking the other way
She turned me off with her putrid smell
Glad I slept looking the other way
I didn't extend my hand around her –
Even with my erotic habits, I couldn't risk lusting for her,
Except to share a bed
Couldn't imagine my skin spinning in delight
She was going to give this loner, strange *siekte*
Bad take-away from a cheap oven
Next day I woke up with a hangover from her pungent smell
I washed my blankets with detergents
Dried them for two days
But she was better than the run-down whore
I once picked up
Who the next day wanted to move in with me
Without any *ndzovolo*
Couldn't tell her there's no honey left in her pot

I really treasure the women I loved:
Onica was a clean and beautiful thief with a trendy hairdo.
She knew the perfume to attract the Bila bee
Loved the songs of Beyonce, R Kelly and TP
She broke into my apartment
And stole my radio and clothes
She left a voice message on my mobile phone:
So you think you are smart? God be with you.
When she received calls while we were eating out
She would say, "I'm with my husband"
Her fingers pressing against my palm
There was no reason to worry about another man

I thought she was a respectable woman fit for marriage
But I was her sex trash bin
Her ATM

Mpume rode in lux buses from KwaMashu to Polokwane
We went to poetry readings and book launches together in Jozi
But when I wanted a baby, all I could get was drop
The Malawian healer gave me something bitter to cook
It was smelling, ready to give me TB
I threw the *muthi* onto Pietersburg Primary school grounds at night
Her cousin notified me of her death eight years later
I should have attended her funeral and met her son Manqoba
Rest in peace my friend

My one night stands were a disaster
At 23, I slept with two prostitutes in Hillbrow
Flaxman introduced me to the Little Rose, it was a dangerous place
Most men have walked in and out of brothels
A prostitute searched my pants, stole all my notes
Whilst I was busy with another one
In another encounter, I couldn't get an erection
I had to pay still and there was no change
That's why I no longer enter brothels

At 24, I travelled to Harare by Translux bus on my own
Marjorie Jobson had invited me
To the prestigious African Human Rights camp
I saw pictures of Mugabe lined up on the road to the airport
Dictator I thought, but it was none of my business
His people want him to rule forever
Or is it true that the dead can vote for Uncle Bob in Zim?

I arrived late and slept at the Earlside hotel
There were faeces under the double bed of old unwashed linen
A prostitute knocked, it was late in the night
I wouldn't open the door, I hadn't invited her

I had been warned thousands die of Aids in Zim
I suffered from flu for three weeks
There's a permanent Zim scar on my face from that vicious flu

I met a woman who was horny, I was horny too
But when I noticed her black clothes, I knew she was a widow
I curtailed all movements of my flesh
Scared to die of *makhuma*

I saw married course participants removing their rings for young boys
I met Anglican priests who smoked and drank unashamedly
And still made sense as they spoke fondly
About heaven on earth – about liberation theology
I went to Chinhoyi caves, admired the pool of cobalt blue water
Some white ultra divers dived deep into the pool
I feared the spirits would capture me, curse me for good
In Zambezi River I feared to be grabbed
By Nyaminyami, the river god of the Tonga
But Nyaminyami deals with the adventurous clan
That dares to see what's beneath the mud
I returned home safe
With a wooden sculpture and a drum from Harare

X

I've been a poet since I was 17
Poetry has been my passport to countries around the world
My poetry is published in ten or fifteen languages
It is used in foreign universities
Quoted in papers, magazines, newspapers, dissertations and books
Researchers from far visit to make films about me
But in my South Africa, in my Xitsonga, my books are foreign
And there's no library or bookshop to keep them safe in my village

I've read my poems in Tampere, Turku and Helsinki
But Lahti Poetry Week was special, I read poems by the lake

Old male poets played horns, flutes, trumpets and trombones
They sang their sorrows with precision accompanied by the *kantele*
At the Lahti library my books were displayed everywhere
When I read my poems an old man read
The translated Finnish version
Though I never told him which poems I was going to read.

On May 2009, the South African ambassador to Finland
H.E. Mr Sobizana Mngqikana invited me
To read poems at his official residence in Katajaharjuntie
He nodded as I condemned corruption in ANC-led government
He nodded as if to say
It's an unintended consequence of the revolution
He gave me a Black Label Scotch whisky
A week earlier he gave the same bottle to bra Hugh Masekela
'I know artists. Don't tell me you don't drink, sober like a judge.'
Walking in Helsinki, travelling in trams and buses
Made me feel like the only black on earth
But the Finns were nice to me
It's just that I come from an apartheid land
Where everything is in black and white

At 30, upon landing in Addis Ababa
A rogue took me around the city, he organized a metered taxi
I paid, we went to Abyssinia hotel –
The guide called it house of culture
But I saw a stinking brothel
Girls made strong coffee from ground beans
They danced to reggae tracks happily
They invited me to dance with them

I bought them wine and paid 200 dollars for a bottle of champagne
It was ridiculous, daylight robbery
We left Abyssinia brothel with two prostitutes to the Ghion hotel
One for Bila, the other for Thami my shy comrade from Cape Town
The hotel management demanded cash to give girls access to our rooms

I was tired and didn't have dollars for one round
I'm lucky I wasn't strangled by prostitutes
I'm lucky I attended the African Social Forum
And helped them start the paper *African Flame*

In Ghana, novelist Niq Mhlongo nicknamed me Banku
Because I ate *banku* and tilapia every day for three weeks
Sandile Ngidi called me Samson because of my long dreadlocks
At the Elmina slave castle at Cape Coast
Black Americans wept when they heard
How slaves were whipped to death
Women forced to have sex with the governor
How the strong men got into ships of gloom
And sailed on the Atlantic to work on plantations
To build infinite cities, churches and bridges
Driven like bellowing bulls to the dipping hole
It was necessary to weep
I was close to tears
I shouted, Reparations now!
Because after reading *The Beautyful Ones Are Not Yet Born*
I agree with Ayi Kwei Armah
Just like Manu Herbstein's novel *Ama: Atlantic Slave Trade*
The fruits of liberation are still to be harvested
Nothing efflorescent here
Hungry children dangle on the backs of women
Though traders sell fish, yam, cassava, cocoa and kente at the market
Hayikhona, nothing efflorescent here

At 37, I went to Algeria
Libya the neighbour was burning
Gaddafi: wanted dead or alive
I grew up adoring his green book
But he had now earned the stripes of a tyrant
They killed him in the Battle of Sirte
That's what occupied my mind in Algiers

At Tipaza ruins
I was reminded of ancient Mapungubwe and the living gods
I washed my feet at the silver-plated Mediterranean sea
I wanted to visit Frantz Fanon's grave, but next time

At the Algiers Book Fair people carried
Brown paper bags full of books
In my country, politicians seldom set foot in bookshops and libraries
Those who push trolleys and carry big bags
Are from supermarkets in the mall
I didn't see a tavern or bottle store in the city of Algiers
They say Algeria is a police state, but I liked it
Children go to school, otherwise they're punished
No one dies in a stampede seeking education
Algeria, beautiful land of omnivorous readers

The Berbers were invisible, yet it's their land till the Sahara
The Berbers sent the French packing
Now they fight against the Arabization of their lives
I stayed away from Muslim women
Can't touch them like we do in Mzantsi

XI

At 35, Mhlahlandlela my son was born in Polokwane
There was load shedding in town
Lights on and off, that's Eskom, we know
Ag shame big brother Joe, why did you think *ndzi biwe hi xitluka*
That I could never have children on this earth?
I rushed to see him a few minutes after his birth
He had scales on feet and hands
He cried full of jubilance when I took pictures of him
He was born ten days later than the gynaecologist had predicted
I walked home proudly
Framed the photo I took when he was twelve minutes old
Today I read him bedtime stories

We compose songs and beat the drums together
And he tells me everything about Tom and Jerry
He calls himself Ben Ten
He works methodically, packs everything orderly
He calls me and granny ancients who were born in Gazankulu
At Mahonisi Combined School, his girlfriend is Ofentse
The smart girl from Vleifontein
One day he gave her R5, perhaps to buy *magwinya*
Then she kissed his forehead in class
This guy passes English and Maths so well
The Zimbabwean teacher Ms Phamela says he can't read Xitsonga –
The language of his father
He sits at the back, too shy to speak in class
He gives his friend Blessing some cash –
It's a protection fee against the rude boys
He's tiny, with no strength to wrestle the bully crocs
He rarely speaks Tshivenda, his mother tongue
But when he visits granny Tshililo at Tshitereke, he's got no choice
In Polokwane, he went to an Afrikaans crèche
He learnt *kom hierso, vat hierso* and remembers his friend Bertus
When he's big, he wants to be a police officer in Polokwane
He'll arrest the criminals
Ignore their nightly melancholy songs behind bars
He'll save some money and buy two cars:
A Subaru sports sedan and a taxi
We'll take a game drive to Kruger Park as a family
He'll give daddy the Subaru
But daddy can't drive
Eyes can't see in the dark

At 37, my second son Samora was born
He was premature, weighing 2.6 kg
Some children are born weighing just a kilo
With a head of a bird
I lost weight before his birth
At four months, Tshivhula the gynaecologist said

74

The child's blood and mother's are different
I lost weight when I heard the sad news
Her friend Matome and boyfriend Thabo rushed Gudani
To Moria for prayers and injunctions
Elderly women washed her at Ritruda with sand and salt
But she didn't stop going to western doctors
She's a woman of steel
Today Samora is a big boy of four
He walks with chest out like a soldier
He eats everything, all the time
But his tummy is flat
His brain is razor sharp
He sings:
Modimo a le teng   (Where God resides)
Gago na mathatha   (There's ever no problem)
Modimo a le teng   (Where the Almighty resides)
Gago na makaka   (There's ever no shit)
He bursts into laughter
Hahaha, hehehe!
He watches me take a bath
Scan me through carefully
He bursts into laughter:
Papa, your pipi is fat
Mine is thin
Hey papa, you've got a beard everywhere
A beard growing in your armpits and groin!
One day he'll speak properly
He's got nicknames for everyone in the house
He calls himself pastor Mubi – the warrior
He fights non-stop like Samora Maxele the revolutionary
Always running in the house, breaking things
Bigger boys can't steal his play toys
When I sometimes smack his backside, or pinch him
He'll smile and say *a swi vavi*   (it's not painful)
Then he'll kick my face, give me a hot *klap*
It's wrestling all the way

When he grows up, he says he wants to be a robot
No, he shakes his head
No, a soldier or police officer
Hands up! Licence!
He'll buy mama and papa each a BMW convertible
Xilahla-matende
He'll drive a motorbike to visit his girlfriend Ndzalo at Waterval
Every night he demands a bedtime story
I tell him the story of Nyiko and Russel
Who go fishing at Dombani Dam
Nyiko catches fish; Russel catches frogs, snakes and a croc
He demands this unwritten story every night
Then we pray together before he retires to bed
But lights must be up
With load shedding – Eskom so powerless
Failing to keep lights on, he's in trouble
Tears are always rolling down his cheeks
Scared of darkness, scared to be stolen
Like thugs stealing power cables
Like government felons stealing the sun

At 42, Masase was born at Louis Trichardt Memorial Hospital
Weighing 2.2 kg
With that smile, even when asleep –
She'll turn heads of boys asunder
When she walks across the boulevards
And alleys of the universe
Two male doctors and two female nurses pulled her out
from her mother's womb
Vha nkokodzekanya vha nga vha sa mvisa na mala thumbuni (They
pulled as if the intestines would come out)
Vha nkhwikhwidza ha nga hu ḓo bva na zwiṅwe zwi so ngo ḓaho
(Pulling as if something uncalled for would burst out)
Nga tshavho vhe ni songo vhona u naka ha muthu nga nnḓa (Don't be
deceived by the beauty of a human being from outside)
Ngomu ha muthu ho ṱangana-ṱangana (Inside a person it's a mess)

Muvhili wanga a u ngo ḓowela u khurumedza   (My body is not used to pushing, pushing)
Thumbu yanga a i tatamuwi a i fonyani sa shonzha   (My stomach does not stretch and shrink like a mopani worm)
Thaṅwe ndi na dumbu la munna   (Perhaps I have a belly of a man)
Lo no tatamuwa lo oma li sa gabagabi   (Firm and un-elastic)

Shedding skin after skin, is utmost love
Masase, I call her *makhadzi*
She'll give us grandchildren
Bright little eyes
Granny calls her *n'wantlhadyana*, a bright hare
Great-granny *vho*-Meresi came to salute her
Though her feet are unsteady
She took a taxi from Vufhuli to Shirley
To sing songs of life to you
She carried a basket of finely crushed maize on her head
A big bowl of *dini* well covered against flies
A case of cool drinks
A shawl to shelter Masase her great grandchild
against the wind and diseases
She knelt down before *maseve*, hands covering her head, *aaa!*
My mother sang and danced
We clapped and sang along:
Thimbya rimbya thimbya rimbya   (Oh, what a wonder)
Ku veleka vukosi   (Giving birth is wealth)
Thimbya rimbya thimbya rimbya   (Oh, what a wonder)
Ku veleka vukosi   (Giving birth is wealth)
I asked *vho*-Meresi what she had brought for me
She giggled: We gave you a wife to caress
I danced as mama sang jubilantly
Va navela vambuya, ku saseka ka swona   (How marvellous it is, the childless are envious)
Va navela vambuya, ku saseka ka swona   (How marvellous it is, the childless are envious)

XII

In July 2010 I sent *ndzovolo* to the Ramikosi family
Far away in Tshitereke, at the end of Limpopo
I sent my aunt Sylvia, my brother Philly,
Buti Piet Jonas, *sesi* Conny Shisana
They brought Gudani my black beauty home dressed in nwenda
Well, she's sometimes sulky and casual
She's the one who danced domba at Ha-Tshivhase
And sung:
Luṱanga lu a songolowa musi vhana vha tshi lima   (A river reed
zigzagging, while children have ploughed)
Ahee, ahee   (Yeah, yeah)
Vhavenda women beat the drums and danced *malende*
Matakadza mbilu ndi ṅwana   (That which pleases the heart is a child)
Ahehe, ahe, ndi ṅwana   (Yeah, yeah, it's a child)
Matakadza mbiluni ndi ṅwana   (That which pleases deep inside is a
child)
A-shoo shoo baby, ndi ṅwana   (Hush, hush baby, it's a child)
There was so much food and beer
The whole village came to feast
We ate *tihove* and sliced pumpkins
Vhavenda looked at the expanse of my ancestral land –
And the green fields of growing spinach, tomatoes and onions –
They realized their daughter wouldn't starve
But I'm glad she's not a *nyankwavi* –
Nestled in a bed of clean white cotton linen
Flickering eyes hold each other
Her bubbly breasts my pillow
Oh, she can weave a dance
Dance gently undisturbed all the fire dances
Dance to the everlasting rippling sounds of our long drum beat
Dum de dum dum, dum de dum dum
Dance as the oiled loins move rhythmically to the starlit melodies
Dance until the vigorous rain comes down
Look at our handsome boys and gorgeous girl

The ancestors are smiling, they are dancing
And I call on them not to bend, but defend this family
Protect our feet from cracking in the dew of invisible thorns
Let your children not eat the sweltering, sweating sand
Let the pots in the kitchen simmer with steamed pap and vegetables
We don't eat roaches and termite in this house
We don't cook stones for supper in this house

I've been going to the gym since 27
But I hardly lose weight and fat
Because I eat a mountain of pap every day
Plate piled up to the ceiling with pap and boerewors
I sit in the steam bath,
Talk about women, corruption and fraud in Limpopo, and football
Clean-shaven tall men freely dangle their AK 47s
I watch the slim girls in tracksuits and tights jog on the tread mill
My wife likes her cake and Cola
Big and elegant cars are parked outside
I walk to Ritruda flat on Thabo Mbeki Street
There's beauty in walking
But one day, and very soon, this communist will drive a Benz

XIII

At 40, I asked my wife
To burn the thirteen-year-old dreadlocks on my head
Not because I was honouring the dead
Nor was I scared of thugs in Pretoria
Who can kill a man for dreadlocks
To beautify black women's heads who love African locks and braids
Nor was I slaving in Tomboni jail
It had been nice to wear dreadlocks –
Girls dipped their fingers in dreads in salons
I danced on stage like a sangoma in a trance
Artists loved me
Christians judged me

Airport police always ambushed me
Confusing me for a criminal on the run

At 38, every part of my body itched
I scratched my body for the whole night
My manhood shrunk
The wolf was knocking on the door
Perhaps I was paying the price for building a writers' village
In the sea of poverty
My brother Simon took me to Moria
But I couldn't enter the holy place
With dangling dreadlocks and a beard

Two years later, I bled through my pipe
Two days before that, three men in black suits visited my house
They said they were preaching the word of God
Visiting every house in the village
They had their own type of Bible which they wanted to read
I told them to leave my house in peace
They said they were members of Jehovah's Witness
My brother's son Hluli asked them to look at the ZCC badge
On my mother's chest on their way out
They remained seated on the sofas
They wanted to convert all of us to their church
But eventually they left
I don't want to see these belligerent charlatans again

I don't know what's growing in my blood
All I know is that I'm not getting any younger
I drink lots of fresh water, biter raw aloe juice, moringa,
African potato and rooibos tea
I drink buchu, camomile, ginseng and green tea
Like the long living Chinese and Japanese
My diet is garlic and ginger and lemon,
Thanks to the whisky boozing Dr Beetroot
I eat lots of *xibavi* and *nkaka* and *guxe* that grows in my garden

Because I want to be a man even at 90
And if I can break the record of world's oldest person I wouldn't mind
But I'm scared of organ failure
Or let's say a kaput penis
Or to be so old and covered with fresh cow dung in the mornings
Dried out in the sun
So that muscles can't move
No, I don't want to be a fairytale
A tourist attraction for those who wish to see
The oldest living person in Elim

Like Hippocrates, the father of modern medicine
I believe in sage herbs and roots that heal
Like King Solomon the poet
I believe in the vegetal alchemy resources that exist in Africa
The aromatic barks and bulbs that heal

My medical history is not colourful
And I don't want it to be colourful
I've never spent a night chained in a mental hospital
Nor lain unconscious, wired in a life support machine
One man got a good job after years of eating ash
Then became diabetic from enjoying his cash and salacious dishes
And when the pains and aches attacked his obese body
Doctors ordered the man to get rid of the saturated fat and salt
Run in the treadmill brother, burn in the steam bath
Stop braaing and boozing brother
Now the tycoon eats cabbage and salads
Perhaps he feels deprived of the good life

Though I don't paint my lungs with smoke
Nor live in taverns of arthritic bingeing wheezing ravens
I'm shit scared of cancer and Aids
Mugabe, with or without a nappy,
Flies over to Singapore for treatment
Mandela is rushed to a private clinic in Pretoria

Bara is crowded
Corpses on sale
Undertakers book corpses in broad daylight
My pockets have holes – I have no medical aid
My wife is unemployed
My mother a pensioner
My father is dead
My children are still small
I can't afford to be bed-ridden, eaten by bugs and parasites
Many patients don't return
When they go to that sewer called hospital

My medical history is not colourful
And I don't want it to be colourful
At 40, hematuria made me learn to pray
I grew shingles and dermatitis –
My stomach burnt, veins pained
I suffered cramps when I jogged
Air-filled stomach growled, it was full of foul smoke
Dr Flip van As from Polokwane tried to fix the symptoms
I don't think he dealt with the malaise
But I'm still standing, erect like Rivolwa mountain

At 28 my brother said I was skinny like an Aids frame
Meaning my shoulders were like a clothes hanger
At 38 I took an HIV test
The nurse from Liberty Life came to Timbila office
To squeeze my blood
Negative. Hooray!
It wasn't for the first time
I did my first HIV test at 27
Every time I take out a life cover, my blood is squeezed by pathologists
I thank God and my ancestors for keeping me breathing
In my country people don't live long –
Those who live long are whites and black bourgeoisie with medical aid
When I feel feeble and weak

Others join the brothers in monasteries
And become monks who reflect in silence
I just want to be soaked in Kwenani River
That's where papa and mama got baptised

At 41, May Day
I took the R71 to Moria
Across the mountain, down the slopes
I followed the star of *Thaba ya Sione*
The mountain comrade Mandela sought prayers
After Robben Island
To dismantle the chains of racial oppression
In a land without moral gravitas
To forge racial reconciliation and peace
In a country where a white assassin murdered Hani
To snuff out the fires of De Klerk decapitating lives
In his Inkatha-inspired township slaughter
I followed the star of *Thaba Sione*
The star that unbent the waist
Of my sister Julia who for three years couldn't walk

On May Day, proletarians and peasants
The reds and greens
Anarchists and gays
Marched upright
Chanting *hau hau*
The future is socialism
Demanding a living wage
Calling for an end to labour brokers
Daring to end the e-tolls in Gauteng
They marched upright
Hand in hand with the Palestinians
Demanding that Obama free the prisoners of Guantanamo Bay
I was not there
But my heart is welded to their just struggle

As my comrades marched in cities' revolutionary squares
I was dizzy
Something was clotting my chest
Choking and gasping for breath
That's why I cut my dreadlocks and a beard
Followed the ubiquitous star of Mount Zion
That's why I was soaked three times in cold Kwenani River:
In the name of the Father, Son and Holy Spirit
And I became closer to Marx, Engels and Lenin
I became one with Fanon, Garvey and Biko
And my culture and this new home are one
Kgotso a e be le lena (Peace be with you)

Now without dreadlocks or a beard
I wear a khaki button-up jacket and cap
I dance *mokhukhu* with the strong army of men
The earth trembles
I leap up and down
Stamping the ground hard with the white *manyanyata* boots
And I'm not drunk, have never tasted beer since I was born
Unless Joko tea and *mogabolo* have intoxicating properties

XIV

Though I'm not a limnologist
Nor a student of potamology
I walk through bushes to follow sounds of waterfalls downstream
I know the braided Mukomadi River
That runs through the swampy Levubu valley
That's where mama collected *hlangasi* grass to make brooms
Brooms she sold at the Elim market to fight hunger
I know rivers along the plains
Rivers creating gorges
I know sources, doors and mouths of rivers of life
Bubbling rivers and gurgling streams
Milambu leyi tsuvulaka misisi yi yima   (Dreadful rivers)

84

Matsolo ya dzunga, ya gudlagudla   (Sour shaky knees)
Ndzi tiva na ribuwo laha ku nekiwaka mapalu na tinjeti   (I know a
river bank where mapalu and tinjeti are dried out)
Mancomani ya ri karhi ya vinjana endzeni ka mati   (Throbbing drums
under water)
Ndzhundzhu yi hiverile, mpfaa, ematini ya ntima dzwii!   (A fully
adorned water snake sauntering on deep dark waters)
Ndzi tiva xihlovo xa ntshava lexi phyaka no hanya hi nkarhi wun'we
(I know a mountain stream that flows and stops simultaneously)
Laha nyoka ya ntshava yi timulaka kona torha   (From where the
mountain snake quenches its thirst)
Laha ku nga lo khwixi, vahloti va thumbhaka na matoto ya mbujani
(In the dense thicket, where hunters pick up droppings of a mountain
snake)

Without dreadlocks or a beard
I look for all types of water to see the next day
I gather and splash with the cold waters of the waterfalls
Drink the clear mountain stream water with delight
Collect the hidden waters of the Mucirindzi well
And the still waters of the meandering Ritavi
I do all it takes to see my children grow fresh and strong
One day they'll finish school and work
Walk up the aisle smiling
Smartly dressed with a suit and a neck-tie

I know where still and flowing water separate each other
I know the mixtures of chicory coffees and teas with salt
And what they do to keep me lean, strong and virile
I know how to wash with salt and coffees
Smear my feet with salt and Vaseline petroleum jelly
I sit in *xixambu* and enjoy the steam of vapour
To scare off nails that want to shoot my feet, drifting to my heart

I no longer eat pork, *timenemene* and *masonja*
Here I don't smoke or drink beer

Sometimes I long for bacon in a hotel breakfast
But there's a lot to eat in the world besides pork
For eating pork is like eating human flesh

Without dreadlocks or a beard
I know how to be pricked with that needle by *baruti*
On my feet and hands
To get rid of the impure blood
I fear the God of Mount Zion
More than my beautiful church uniform and shining emblem
More than the stream water and the sauna
More than the coffees and tea mixtures

I'm learning to pray midnight and early in the morning
I submit my heart to God of Mount Zion
I cherish love, respect, hard work and honesty
I'm a Zionist Christian, not a Christian Zionist
I have nothing against Palestine
I salute the Palestinians' fight against Apartheid Israel

I'm an African
I feel safe in an African church led by an African prophet
Here, we dance and sing familiar songs
We chant *mpoho*, the classical poem
Because *mpoho a se kosha ke thapelo*
I'm visited upon by dreams I can't ignore
For in a world populated by witches and wicked people
You eat from the same bowl with your own relatives at your own risk

XV

I'm lucky to have ZCC prophets who pack news of my future
I'm no longer scared when I see prophets
Squealing, grunting and swinging their faces
Now it's my turn to perform injunctions
Dogs are barking, snorting in the night cunningly

It's my turn to remove the teeth
Of lions and jackals growling on my stoep
Hush, it's my turn to perform injunctions
To clip the wings of agile mating owls
To cut the tails of woolly dogs
To close the creaking door of the dark, open abyss

My faith in the God of Mount Zion is unwavering
The God of Engenas, Edward and Barnabas Lekganyane
Who gives the poor rain and life
The loving God of Risimati, Dayimani and Jonas
The same God of Abraham, Jacob and David
Will keep my heart beating under my ribs
Until the next soothing dream
Until I'm grey and old like Methuselah, Noah, Lamech,
Shem, Isaac and Moses
Until another spring and summer
From sunrise to sundown

Marxism and Black Consciousness are good but not enough
I need protection from my ancestors and God
Though I can't create my own deity
Kae Morii, a Japanese poet and palm reader, once told me to be careful
She said that if I want to live longer
I must take care of my health in my fifties
I asked her how long she would live
Unflinchingly, she said, 120 years
Like Moses the biblical figure

Year upon year, my leaves won't wither too cheaply
I will be walking the streets of the city erect
Walking the paths of my village upright
A collector of tales in taxis and buses and aeroplanes
A collector of myths in rivers and mountains and forests
I will be standing, an immortal word warrior

Glossary

And hi yena papantsongo wa Frank: Xitsonga: And it's him, Frank's uncle.

A ka ha ri vusiku: Xitsonga: I was in the dark, meaning I hadn't started having sex.

Banku: Ghanaian: pap.

Baruti: Sepedi: priest.

Bredie: Originally associated with the Cape Malays and the Dutch, *bredie* is a stew made with mutton, and its seasonings include cinnamon, ginger and chilli.

Buchu: A flowering plant known for its fragrance and medicinal use.

Droëwors: Afrikaans for "dry sausage" is a South African snack food, based on the traditional, coriander-seed spiced boerewors sausage.

Dzelehani: An tiny animal that cries like a baby at night, usually regarded as a bad omen. Sometimes called a bush baby.

Eka: Xitsonga preposition for *at*.

Emachihweni: A village the head of which has died.

Emaxubini: In the ruins.

Gungu ra tirha: Xitsonga proverb implying 'muti works'. 'Gungu' is a short tree stump / bush cut off.

Hahani: Xitsonga for aunt.

Hlangasi: Xitsonga for grass that grows in swampy areas, usually harvested to make brooms.

Hogo: Traditional circumcision school.

Hogo huwelela: A common song sung at the circumcision camp.

Imbiza: An African medicinal tonic made from the African potato and other ingredients. It is believed that it reduces high blood pressure, clears skin conditions, boosts energy and vitality, helps to clean the womb, and prevents arthritis.

Izikhothane: Derived from the isiZulu word *ukukhothana*, which means 'to lick'. Izikhothane gatherings often culminate in the burning of expensive clothes and money by young people in an act of showing off wealth.

Jozi-mjipa-msawawa: Slang for Johannesburg.

Kantele: A plucked string instrument of the dulcimer and zither family native to Finland and Karelia.

Kenya: A large bundle of woven grass thatch tied in such a way that it can be unrolled on the roof of a hut. Among the Vatsonga, this mat was also used to wrap and preserve the corpse of a poor person who couldn't afford a decent blanket or linen.

Ku fanele ku songiwa masangu: Xitsonga proverb: mats must be folded; meaning sex is prohibited.

Kokwani: Xitsonga: granny.

Kotana: A little stick used by ZCC priests to bless the sick and troubled.

Kwaito: A style of popular music similar to hip hop, featuring vocals recited over an instrumental backing with strong bass lines.

Leswaku swifuva swi ta pfuleka: Xitsonga proverb: so that your chest can open up (so you can remember).

Madala: Nguni [IsiZulu, IsiXhosa, IsiNdebele and IsiSwati]: old man.

Madlala: Circumcision lodge and rites.

Mafufunyani: A state of sudden madness or hysteria.

Magayisa: Xitsonga: migrant workers / workers returning home from town or mines.

Mageu: Light fermented body-boosting drink made of corn.

Majekejeke: Grass or reed used to make sleeping mats.

Makhuma: Illness of men caused by connection with female not yet purified after abortion or confinement; illness due to omission of purification rites after a death.

Makhadzi: Tshivenda: aunt.

Makhwaya: Traditional Tsonga dance for men.

Malende: A traditional Venda dance for both men and women, boys and girls. Unlike tshigombela which is performed on special occasions to praise chiefs, malende can be performed for any happy event.

Malusu: Muthi with a spell that is used in male circumcision camps to make the initiates obliterate thoughts of returning home.

Masonja: Xitsonga: "mopani worms", a delicious dish mainly served in Limpopo province.

Mbogo/Mpoho: A signature song of the ZCC.

Mbhokota: A populated rural village near Elim in Limpopo province.

Mencwa: Misfortunes caused by witches on a targeted victim; in the context of the poem, the two missing brothers.

Mhani: Xitsonga: mom.

Mhani-nkulu: Xitsonga: elder mom / one's mother's sister.

Mi fanele ku biwa hi ximoko: You are supposed to be whipped (often by an animal hide or a sjambok). If a witch or wizard is found trapped in a homestead, they can be whipped so that they leave and go home to die.

Mi fembiwa: An examination carried out by a specialist sangoma/ diviner or prophet to 'smell out', i.e. to detect and remove strange things like wires, lizards, bottles, snakes, etc. injected in one's body by witches.

Milawu: Laws and chants sung in a circumcision school.

Mi rhadzunuriwa: And get de-bewitched/ detoxed / cleansed.

Miroho: Xitsonga: vegetables.

Mugabagaba: A plant with big elephant-like leaves often used for detoxification.

Muhulu: Xitsonga: one's mother's sister.

Mukapu: Xitsonga: soft porridge often prepared for the weak and sick.

Murahelakule: Witch's chemistry aimed at driving a person far away from home forever.

Mushavhanamadi: Tshivenda: a person who does not wash.

Muthi: Medicine, usually traditional.

Mogabolo: Sepedi: holy and blessed ZCC drinking water and tea.

Mokhukhu: Sepedi for a shack dwelling. In this poem, *mokhukhu* refers to the Zion Christian Church's male organised rhythmic dance which is characterised by frequent and collective leaps into the air and coming down stamping their feet on the ground with their white boots called **manyanyatha**. Usually, the *mokhukhu* performances last for hours, with no meals in between, except the drinking of sugarless tea and *mogabolo* (holy and blessed water) before the performance. The *mokhukhu* dancers are usually called *mashole a thapelo*, meaning the soldiers of prayer.

Ndzi biwe hi xitluka: Xitsonga proverb: 'I'm impotent'.

Ndzovolo: Traditional bride-price, formerly paid in cattle, but nowadays given as a cash payment.

Nkuwa wa le kaya eMaphanyini: Xitsonga: the home fig tree at Maphanyini (where buses and taxis drop and go). This fig tree station is also called Lucky.

Nyankwavi: A girl who is not supposed to get married, but feed the xin'wanakaji, alternatively known as tokoloshi.

Nwenda: A colourfully embroidered upper garment made from multi-coloured striped cloth worn by Vhavenda women and girls.

N'wana wa munhu u le kusuhani: The Son of Man is nearby, meaning Jesus is coming.

Pantsula: A fashionable young urban black person, especially a man. Also a dance style in which each person performs a solo turn within a circle of dancers doing a repetitive, shuffling step.

Phala bashimane: Traditional medicine.

Phunyuka bamphethe: African magic spell that enables a thief to escape undetected or causes the court to ignore clear evidence of a crime.

Potjiekos: Afrikaans: "small pot food", a stew prepared outdoors, usually cooked in a three-legged pot.

Sangoma: A traditional healer or diviner.

Sivara: Xitsonga: bother-in-law in Xitsonga.

Swa yila wa yila: Xitsonga: 'a taboo is always a taboo.'

Swibantsheke: A game of sliding down a hill or skating, usually by boys.

Swigirigiri: Cart wheel made of a disc or wood.

Swoswo: Tripe of a goat, sheep or beast.

Ta lava hundzeke emisaveni: For the deceased [a Radio Tsonga programme in the 80s which was aired every night].

Timenemene: Xitsonga: edible flies collected from anthills in summer.

Toyi toyi: A dance step characterised by high-stepping movements commonly performed at political and protest gatherings.

Order of Ikhamanga: A South African honour, instituted in November 2003 and it is granted by the President of South Africa for achievements in arts, culture, literature, music, journalism, and sports.

Ubhejana: A herbal and vegetable concoction which was promoted by post-apartheid South Africa's health minister Dr Manto Tshabalala as a cure for Aids.

Valoyi va pfurhetela leswaku mi nga voni ndlela ya le kaya: Xitsonga: witches blow evil spirit so that you become forgetful, and do not think of home.

Vadzabi: Xitsonga: traditional circumcision mentors and carers of the initiates.

Vaveni: Xitsonga: tokoloshe, evil spirit or voodoo.

Vho-: Tshivenda: added to a person's name as a title of respect, e.g Mr or Mrs in Tshivenda.

Wa: Xitsonga: preposition *of*, often meaning means *the son of.*

Xidyisa: Xitsonga: something harmful one has been made to eat without knowing, such as poison, a drug or a magic ingredient.

Xifula: Xitsonga: a cancerous wound, stroke or any sudden and unusual incurable medical condition allegedly believed to be planted in people by wicked people and witches.

Xifuva xaku xi file xana?: Xitsonga meaning 'is your chest dead?'; meaning 'can't you remember anything?'

Xihlungwani: Xitsonga: a carved wooden crown or cover of thatch that is used to close the top of hut roof. Among the Vatsonga, when the head of a family dies, the *xihlungwani* is removed to indicate that he is no more; and the place is usually referred to as *emachihweni,* meaning the place of lawlessness.

Xilahla-matende: Xitsonga: an open roof, convertible car

Xirimela: The Pleiades, which rise at hoeing time.

Xivonelo: Cone-shaped portion of porridge brought by women to feed those in circumcision camp.

Xiwacha: Mixtures of earth, sea water and other ingredients believed to have potent powers to cure and exorcise evil spirits. Xiwacha is often used by members of the Apostolic Zionist church.

Xixambu: Xitsonga: vapour bath.

Xi nga ri na nhonga xi sila hi mandla: He who crushes [tobacco] without a mortar and pestle but with bare hands.

7/8 u ya lithanda isaka la mazambani / U ya lithanda isaka la mazambani: An IsiZulu song that my father Daniel Risimati Bila loved with passion. The composer is not known, but the song was performed by a male song and dance troupe during his school days at Shirley Agricultural and Industrial School for Natives, and during the potato tasting festivities organised by the Swiss missionary and liberal, Herbert Stanley Phillips and his wife Lucette Phillips, at Shirley farm.

Acknowledgements

This collection could not have been completed in its current form without generous assistance from many individuals. My deepest thanks go to my mother, Fokisa N'wa-Mahatlani Maxele for her sharp memory even at the age of 80. Her unparalleled ability to remember matters of rich social and family history without any scholarly reference to any journal is remarkable. Although she doesn't yearn to be called a poet, her voice is defiantly present in these poems. It is not accidental; my mother is a real poet without official certification.

The original versions of five of these poems were mostly written as part of my 2013 MA in Creative Writing at Rhodes University. I'm therefore indebted to my supervisors and practising poets Mxolisi Nyezwa and Robert Berold for their invaluable suggestions and critical comments on the poems, and their conviction that poetry is 'a labour of passion, full of energy,' where every word, line and stanza is weighed to create blended music, clear images and internal logic. It was Berold who suggested that I put together this collection of longer poems. I hope the desired inherent value of this poetry lives in voice and print, stage and page.

I thank Spree MacDonald, Vuyisile Msila and Mark Waller for their invaluable comments on my poems. Your critical feedback is always appreciated.

Denis Hirson was attracted to *Ancestral Wealth*, perhaps because of the multiplicity of languages in it or its ancestral theme. He invited me over to Paris in 2013 as part of 2013 South Africa French Seasons to read poetry together with other South African poets at the Festival international de poetes en Val de Marne, organised by Francis Combes and Nelly George-Picot whom I thank dearly. Particular thanks also go to Brigitte Daian and Carole Durand of the Maison de la poesie Rhone-Alpes, who invited me and Gabeba Baderoon to read poetry in Grenoble. I read the poem *Ancestral Wealth*, and Brigitte Daian gave a spellbinding rendition of the French version translated by J.P Richard. She sung words off the pages and I gracefully bowed before her. Later the same poem in French translation was published widely, notably in the anthology *Pas de blessure, pas d'histoire*, edited by Denis Hirson, which was a special edition of the review *Bacchanales*.

I am indebted to the poetic wisdom of Nazim Hikmet, whose classic poem *Autobiography* gave shape to my own life story.

For consent to use previously published poems in this collection, acknowledgement is made to the following:

"Ancestral wealth": first appeared in *Tyhini* (ISEA, 2012), *The Sol Plaatje European Union Poetry Anthology Vol III*, (Jacana Media, 2013), *In the Heat of Shadows*, edited by Denis Hirson, (Deep South, 2014).

"Boys from Seshego": *New Coin*, Vol. 48 No 1, (June 2012) and received second prize for The Sol Plaatje European Union Poetry Award.

"Images from childhood" first appeared under the title "Memory": *Timbila 7*, (September 2013), and received second prize for The Sol Plaatje European Union Poetry Award.

"Missing": *New Coin*, Vol.43 No. 2 (December 2007), *Timbila 6*, (September 2008), and *We Have Crossed Many Rivers* edited by Dike Okoro, Malthouse.

"N'wa-Yingwani": first appeared under the title "shovels clatter" in *New Coin* vol. 48 No 2, (December 2012).

"Why I am not a teacher": *New Coin* vol. 50 No 2, (December 2014).

Printed in the United States
By Bookmasters